WHY WOMEN
KILL THEMSELVES

WHY WOMEN KILL THEMSELVES

Edited by

DAVID LESTER, Ph.D.

Professor of Psychology
Richard Stockton State College
Pomona, New Jersey

CHARLES C THOMAS • PUBLISHER
Springfield • Illinois • U.S.A.

Published and Distributed Throughout the World by

CHARLES C THOMAS • PUBLISHER
2600 South First Street
Springfield, Illinois 62794-9265

© *1988 by* CHARLES C THOMAS • PUBLISHER
ISBN 0-398-05508-4
Library of Congress Catalog Card Number: 88-16018

With THOMAS BOOKS *careful attention is given to all details of manufacturing*
and design. It is the Publisher's desire to present books that are satisfactory as to their
physical qualities and artistic possibilities and appropriate for their particular use.
THOMAS BOOKS *will be true to those laws of quality that assure a good name*
and good will.

Printed in the United States of America
Q-R-3

Library of Congress Cataloging in Publication Data
Why women kill themselves / edited by David Lester.
    p. cm.
    Includes bibliographies and index.
    ISBN 0-398-05508-4
    1. Suicide. 2. Women--Suicidal behavior. I. Lester, David,
1942-
    [DNLM: 1. Suicide--psychology. 2. Women--psychology. HV 6546
W629]
RC569.W48   1988
616.85′8445′0088--dc19
DNLM/DLC
for Library of Congress   88-16018
                                       CIP

CONTRIBUTORS

Dorothy Ayers Counts, Ph.D.

Professor of Anthropology
University of Waterloo
Waterloo, Ontario, Canada

Antoon A. Leenaars, Ph.D., C. Psych.

Windsor, Ontario, Canada

David Lester, Ph.D.

Professor of Psychology
Richard Stockton State College
Pomona, New Jersey

Charles Neuringer, Ph.D.

Professor of Psychology
University of Kansas
Lawrence, Kansas

B. Joyce Stephens, Ph.D.

Associate Professor of Sociology
State University College of New York
Fredonia, New York

Bijou Yang, Ph.D.

Assistant Professor of Economics
Drexel University
Philadelphia, Pennsylvania

For Carol Ammons
for her encouragement

PREFACE

MANY RESEARCH findings in the study of suicide are hard to replicate. One published study may find a particular phenomenon, while another may fail to find the same phemonenon or may produce results that qualifies the earlier conclusion.

One of the clearest phenomenon in suicidal behavior is the difference in the suicidal behavior of the sexes. Males complete suicide at a higher rate than females while females attempt suicide at a higher rate than males. This difference has been known for centuries and has been consistently reported. An early explanation was that women used less lethal methods for suicide than men, but this is easily shown not to be the sole answer for, within any one method, men die more and women survive more.

Since the roles of the two sexes differ greatly in most societies and since men and women differ in many psychological characteristics, it is of interest also to inquire whether the meaning of suicide for women and the motivation for suicide differ from those of men.

The present book focuses upon these interesting and important issues. The editor and the contributing authors have examined suicidal behavior in women from a variety of perspectives—anthropological, physiological, psychological, and sociological. We cannot tie the conclusions of each chapter together into a neat theoretical package, but we can illustrate the diversity of the possible answers to the problem of why women kill themselves.

In addition, to illustrate the more academic discussions of suicidal behavior in women, we have included two case studies—Virginia Woolf who killed herself and Dorothy Parker who early in her life attempted suicide. Obviously, two women, even these two women, cannot be representative of all or even most women. However, these two women have interested people, and detailed biographies have appeared on them, enabling us to examine their lives in much greater detail than the average woman. These two biographical essays are offered simply to give readers two detailed case studies for examination and for testing their hypotheses about the causes of suicide in women.

David Lester

CONTENTS

Page

Preface ix

Chapter

1. Suicide in Women: An Overview — *David Lester*................... 3
2. An International Perspective — *David Lester* 17
3. The Suicide Rates of Women in America — *David Lester*........... 25
4. Women, Work and Suicide — *Bijou Yang* 35
5. The Thinking Processes in Suicidal Women — *Charles Neuringer*....... 43
6. The Suicide Notes of Women — *Antoon A. Leenaars*................ 53
7. The Social Relationships of Suicidal Women — *B. Joyce Stephens* 73
8. Ambiguity in the Interpretation of Suicide - Female Death in Papua, New Guinea — *Dorothy Ayers Counts* 87
9. Suicide and the Menstrual Cycle — *David Lester*...................111
10. A Physiological Theory of Sex Differences in Suicide — *David Lester* ...119
11. Virginia Woolf - The Life of a Completed Suicide — *David Lester*......125
12. Dorothy Parker - The Life of an Attempted Suicide — *David Lester* 133

Name Index 143
Subject Index 147

xi

WHY WOMEN
KILL THEMSELVES

CHAPTER 1

SUICIDE IN WOMEN: AN OVERVIEW[1]

DAVID LESTER

ONE OF THE most consistent findings from research into suicidal behavior is that males kill themselves more than females. In contrast, females attempt suicide more than males. This sex difference has been found in almost all nations, in almost all eras, and in almost all subgroups of the population of a given nation (for example, in white and black Americans, in the single, widowed, married, and divorced, and in all age groups).

It is very difficult to trace all completed and attempted suicides in a community, but three efforts have been made to do this. Farberow and Shneidman (1961) in Los Angeles in 1957 found 540 men but only 228 women who completed suicide. In contrast, they located 1824 women but only 828 men who had attempted suicide. Yap (1958) studied Hong Kong, whose population is mainly Chinese. He located 145 men but only 118 women who had completed suicide, whereas he located 508 women but only 386 men who had attempted suicide. In the Netherlands, de Graaf and Kruyt (1976) located 731 male and 478 female completed suicides as compared to 1562 male and 2551 female attempted suicides.

Completed Suicide

Data for completed suicides are more easily obtained since these deaths are officially recorded with reasonable accuracy. Looking at mortality statistics, there is an excess of male suicides both across the United States and across the world. The ratio of the male suicide rate for the

---

1. This chapter is based on Lester (1984).

3

female suicide ranged from 2.5 in Delaware to 5.6 in Vermont during 1949-51 (Gibbs and Martin, 1964) and from 1.5 in Japan to 7.4 in El Salvador (Gibbs and Martin, 1964) (The ratio for the U.S. was 3.6.). The ratio of the male suicide rate to the female suicide rate for the United States in 1964 ranged from 2.1 for those aged 35-44 to 14.5 for those aged 85 and older (Lester, 1979).

Although the male-female ratio of completed suicides in the United States remained fairly stable over the last twenty years (see Lester, 1979), the female suicide rate has been increasing recently at a proportionately higher rate than for males, though the female suicide rate remains only about one-third of the male suicide rate.

Burvill (1972) looked at nine nations and found that the female suicide rate had increased in all of them from 1955 to 1965, thereby causing the male-female ratio to decrease. It appears, therefore, that modern society is leading to more suicidogenic stress for females while having no ameliorative effect for males. Gove (1972) also has noted this phenomenon. From 1952-53 to 1962-63, the suicide rate for white males in the United States rose 10 percent, whereas the suicide rate for white females rose 49 percent. (The corresponding increases for black males and black females were 33 percent and 80 percent, respectively.) For nine western industrialized nations, the female suicide rate rose 18 percent, while the male suicide rate rose 2 percent.

This relatively higher increase in the female suicide rate is not, however, found in all age groups. Data reported by Metropolitan Life (1976) and presented in Table 1 show that suicide rates from 1963 to 1973 rose relatively more in females aged 35 and older, and in younger males aged 15 to 34.

Completed Suicide in Professional Women

Among professionals, the sex difference in suicide is much less. In some recent studies, females have been found to have a higher suicide rate than males. For example, female physicians have a higher suicide rate than male physicians (Ross, 1973). In other occupations, such as nurses, chemists, and psychologists, the female suicide rate is greater than for the general female population, though still less than the male suicide rate for those occupations.

This increased suicide rate among female professionals may be caused in part by the role conflicts created for females when they work.

Table 1

MORTALITY FROM SUICIDE 1963-64 to 1973-74
FOR THE U.S. WHITE POPULATION*

| | Death rate per 100,000 | | | | | |
| | 1963-64 | | 1973-74 | | Percent change | |
Age	Male	Female	Male	Female	Male	Female
All ages	17.4	6.2	18.8	7.1	8.0	14.5
15-24	9.2	3.0	17.6	4.5	91.3	50.0
25-34	16.7	7.2	22.6	8.6	35.3	19.4
35-44	22.4	10.7	23.3	12.1	4.0	13.1
45-54	31.8	12.5	28.3	13.9	−11.0	11.2
55-64	38.6	11.0	32.3	11.5	−16.3	4.5
65-74	38.9	9.7	35.9	8.8	−7.7	−9.3
75 and over	52.4	6.7	47.1	6.8	−10.1	1.5

*Source: Metropolitan Life (1976).

Furthermore, professional females may experience greater stress in their work (as a result of sexism) than do males. It also appears that stresses from a career may be more suicidogenic than stresses from other sources.

Attempted Suicide

For attempted suicide, Kessler and McRae (1983) reviewed forty-five studies of attempted suicides from 1940 to 1980 and found that the female/male ratio increased up to 1970, where it peaked, and decreased thereafter.

MARITAL STATUS AND SUICIDAL BEHAVIOR

Gove (1972, 1979) has explored in detail the relationship between marital status and completed suicide for males and females. Since World War II, females have had higher rates of mental illness in the United States, and, in particular, married women have higher rates of mental illness than married men. In contrast, never-married men have higher rates of mental illness than never-married women. Gove concluded that marriage reduces psychiatric stress for males but increases psychiatric stress for females. Marriage is more advantageous for men than for women.

Gove examined the ratio of the suicide rate for never-married/suicide rate for married, an index called by Durkheim (1951) the coefficient of preservation. If Gove's hypothesis is correct, this ratio should be higher for males than for females. For the U.S. for 1959-61 the ratio for males aged 26-64 years of age was 2.0 and for females it was 1.5. Single males were 97 percent more likely to complete suicide than married males, while single females were 47 percent more likely to complete suicide than married females. (Divorce and widowhood also seem to be more disadvantageous for males than for females.) Gove also presented data to show that this same pattern appeared when rates of threatened and attempted suicide were examined. Durkheim's coefficient or preservation was consistently higher for males than for females. According to Gove, "there have been changes in the women's role that have been detrimental to (married) women and that, as marital roles are presently constituted in our society, marriage is more advantageous to men than to women while being single (widowed, divorced) is more disadvantageous" (Gove, 1972, pp. 211-212).

Related to this, Bock and Webber (1972) have noted the extremely high suicide rate of the elderly widower as compared to the elderly widow. They attributed this to a greater social isolation (including more frequent absence of kin and of organizational memberships) among the widowers as compared to the widows, and they documented this with a survey of the elderly in a Florida county. The high incidence of suicide among widowers is very likely to be related to the changes in their roles associated with retirement, whereas there may be more continuity in the roles of the women as they age.

Herman (1977) felt that suicide among divorced women was likely to be common because of their dependency role learned from their past life experiences and the difficulty in learning new roles as an adult, both of which would lead to feelings of helplessness.

CHARACTERISTICS OF SUICIDAL INDIVIDUALS

Studies of suicidal individuals have found them to be less active in their social lives and to have poorer relationships with peers and superiors. Suicidal individuals have been found to resent those upon whom they depend, which inhibits straightforward discussions of personal and interpersonal problems and unfulfilled needs. They are also found to have less confidence in their ability to control their future, especially in interpersonal relationships, and to have less ability to use mature interpersonal strategies (Lester, 1972).

Seriously suicidal individuals have been found to have a lifelong inability to maintain warm and mutually interdependent relationships and to be interpersonally isolated and disengaged (even if married). They tended to make more efforts to change their role prior to their suicidal action than low-risk individuals and to communicate more to their significant others (Lester, 1972).

Clinical impressions of suicidal individuals have focused on difficulties in communicating to significant others just what they want from a relationship and on manipulative intent in the suicidal actions, coupled with frequent rejection from the spouse. It has been hypothesized that suicidal actions can result in part from conscious death wishes on the part of the significant other toward the suicidal partner. Suicidal individuals have been described as taking a demanding, passive-aggressive, and clinging role with their partner (Lester, 1972).

A study of married suicidal individuals (Hattem, 1964) concluded that these individuals were more emotionally unstable, more hypersensitive to rejection, and more critical of the world than their nonsuicidal spouse. They felt weak, dependent, and inferior. In contrast, the spouses felt more self-oriented, exploitive, and competitive, and recognized their need to have relationships with weak others. Hattem described these marriages as submissive-exploitive.

Are the characteristics described above more appropriate to the traditional female role or to the traditional male role? Perhaps females have felt less in control of their future than males, have been more likely to take a demanding, passive-aggressive clinging role, and have felt weaker, more dependent, and more inferior than males.

Wold (1971) proposed 10 types of suicidal individuals, based upon his experience with patients at the Los Angeles Suicide Prevention Center. Two types were characteristic only of women.

1. Discarded women had experienced repeated rejection by men and by their parents. They felt that they were failures as women, but assumed a facade of femininity and had hysterical personalities.
2. Harlequin women eroticized death, seeing death as peaceful and pleasurable. They were masochists and alienated, with a poor self-image and a facade of femininity.

Four other types were primarily women.

3. The chaotic type was psychotic, impulsive, and confused.
4. Middle-age depression characterized another type.
5. The "I can't live without you" type had a passive-dependent but stable life-style. She/he became suicidal in response to a rift in a symbiotic relationship.
6. The "I can't live with you" type was typically involved in a relationship with a person of the same type. Both partners were suicidal and harbored destructive wishes for the other.

Two types are found equally often among men and women.

7. Adolescents with problems in communication with their parents, and identity and dependency problems, often became suicidal. It was not unusual for the parents to have death wishes for their children.
8. The old-and-alone type was typically depressed, was in poor physical health, and had given up on life.

The final two types were characteristic of men.

9. The down-and-out type was a drug and alcohol abuser with a downwardly mobile life course. His self-esteem was low, his health poor, and his interpersonal relationships superficial.
10. The violent type experienced episodes of rage. He drank a lot but was able to hold a steady job and was rarely living alone. However, his rage often led to assaultive and self-destructive behavior.

Several studies have identified consistent differences between male and female suicides. Suicidal women tend to be diagnosed more often as neurotic and with affective disorders rather than as schizophrenic or psychopathic (Davis, 1968). Women tend to be suicidal more often in response to interpersonal problems, whereas men tend to be suicidal more often in response to intrapsychic conflicts and to commit suicide in response to job loss and legal problems (Beck, et al., 1973; Farberow, 1970).

EXPLANATIONS OF THE SEX DIFFERENCE

Methods for Suicide

Women use different methods for suicide than those used by men. Men prefer active methods such as hanging and shooting. Women prefer passive methods such as drugs and poisons. More subtle differences exist. When suicide is committed by firearms, men are more likely to shoot themselves in the head. Lester (1969a) has speculated that women are more concerned with their physical appearance after death and so choose less disfiguring methods for suicide. Evidence exists for this notion in a study conducted by Diggory and Rothman (1961) on the consequences of death feared most. Women reported more concern with their physical appearance after death than did men.

Thus, one explanation for the sex difference in suicidal behavior is that women choose methods for suicide that are less likely to kill. For example, you are more likely to survive a shot in the body than one in the head, and you are more likely to survive a drug overdose than a bullet wound.

Lester (1969a) noted that this explanation, though possibly correct in part, was insufficient because within any method men die more often than women. For example, in Los Angeles in 1957, of 24 men who jumped to their death, 16 succeeded; whereas of 27 women who used jumping, only nine were successful.

Perhaps women choose less lethal methods for suicide because they are less intent on dying. However, choice of method may be affected by socialization. For example, Marks and Stokes (1976) surveyed male and female students and found that males had much more familiarity with firearms when growing up than did females. Southern students had more early experience with firearms than northern students, and this was reflected in the finding that suicide was committed most often using firearms in the South, for both males and females. Perhaps these differences in socialization experiences affect the choice of a method for suicide?

Physiological Explanations

Several studies have explored the relationship between the incidence of suicidal behavior and the phase of the menstrual cycle. It appears that the incidence of completed suicide does not vary significantly over the menstrual cycle, but that attempted suicide is more common during the premenstrual and menstrual phases (Lester, 1979; see Chapter 9). Thus, it is possible that the higher incidence of attempted suicide in women is due to an excess of attempts made during these two phases of the menstrual cycle. (However, we must remember that we do not know whether there is an excess during these two phases or a deficit at the other phases of the menstrual cycle.) This has led to the suggestion that the level of the circulating sex hormones affects the incidence of suicidal behavior.

Pregnant women have been found to have a low rate of suicide. One estimate of the suicide rate for pregnant women was .03 (per 100,000 per year) compared to a rate of about 6 for women in general (Barno, 1967). However, attempted suicide seems to be as common in pregnant women as in nonpregnant women (Whitlock and Edwards, 1968). Clearly, changes in the likelihood of suicide during pregnancy can have many causes. However, since pregnancy does involve changes in the levels of circulating hormones, hormone levels have been suggested as a possible source of the lowered incidence of suicidal behavior in pregnant women.

Along these same lines, Kane, Daly, Wallach, and Keeler (1966) reported using Enovid to treat a suicidal woman, and Lester (1969b) has suggested that women using the birth control pill might have a different suicide rate from other women. However, Vessey, et al. (1985) found that the attempted suicide rate in women on the pill did not differ from the rate of those using an intra-uterine device (though both of these groups had a higher suicide rate than women using a diaphragm). The length of time on the pill was not related to the rate of attempted suicide.

These reports by no means prove that the levels of circulating sex hormones affect the incidence of suicidal behavior in women. Psychological explanations of the associations can easily be provided. However, the reports do raise the possibility of a physiological influence on the suicidal behavior of women.

Psychosis and Mental Illness as an Explanation

Lester (1970) noted that psychotics have higher rates for completed suicide while neurotics have higher rates for attempted suicide. A review of community surveys revealed that males are more prone to psychosis, whereas females are more prone to neurosis. A community survey of a county in Tennessee (Roth and Luton, 1943) and one of a section of Baltimore (Lemkau, et al, 1942) both reported this sex difference. Lester suggested that the sex difference in suicide may be a result of this difference in the incidence of particular psychiatric disorders. Males are more likely to become psychotic and so may be more likely to complete suicide. Females are more likely to become neurotic and so may be more likely to attempt suicide. No adequate test of this hypothesis has yet appeared.

Societal Explanations

There is one explanation of the sex difference in suicidal behavior that has particular importance for a discussion of sex roles and suicidal behavior. Linehan (1973) felt that an important determinant of what happens when a person is in crisis is what alternatives are socially acceptable. She felt that attempted suicide was seen in our society as a weak and feminine behavior, and less available to males. Males, therefore, may be less able to communicate mild levels of distress, suppressing their self-destructive impulses until they are so strong as to precipitate a lethal suicide action.

Linehan tested her ideas by presenting to undergraduate students case studies involving males and females in crisis and varying the characteristics of the patients so that some were portrayed as "masculine" while others were portrayed as "feminine." She found that the students predicted suicide as an outcome more often for males than for females, and also that suicide was the predicted outcome more often for masculine patients than for feminine patients. The students predicted suicide 71 percent of the time for the masculine males, 62 percent of the time for masculine females, 43 percent of the time for feminine males, and 22 percent of the time for feminine females.

This suggests that social sex role stereotypes, which are probably based in part on differences in the social roles and the behavior of males and females in the society, serve to perpetuate those stereotyped roles.

FEMALE SUPPRESSION AND SUICIDE

A discussion of sex roles and their influence on the suicide rate has to include the issue of female suppression in societies. Does the differential status of females in a society have any impact upon their suicide rate?

Stewart and Winter (1977) attempted to explore the characteristics of nations in which females were suppressed and discriminated against. They used a sample of all modern countries and identified 25 possible indices of female suppression and/or discrimination, including such variables as the relative amount of education given to females and the length of time for which females have been able to vote. They used a differential measure of the male-female suicide rate by simply subtracting the female suicide rate from the male suicide rate (rather than using a ratio index). Their results showed that the differential suicide rate between the sexes was *not* related to the indices of female suppression/discrimination.

(Incidentally, Stewart and Winter did find that the male suicide rate was relatively higher in countries where the divorce rate was higher, where there were a relatively high number of teenage females married, where there were fewer illegitimate births, where the life expectancies of both sexes were more similar, and where the differences in the male and female homicide rates were less.)

Related to the concept of female suppression is that of ascribed status. Typically, those individuals discriminated against and oppressed in a society have their status ascribed to them. They are what they are and do what they do because of the social roles and societal status prescribed for them. In contrast, the roles of the elite in a society are determined to a large extent by what they themselves accomplish and achieve.

People in ascribed roles have more external constraints on their behavior. Henry and Short (1954) argued that strong external constraints provide a clear external source to blame for one's misery and so facilitate homicidal behavior and inhibit suicidal behavior. In contrast, those in achieved roles have weak external constraints on their behavior. Their failures cannot be blamed so easily on external agents. They themselves must bear the burden of responsibility. Thus, suicidal behavior is facilitated and homicidal behavior is inhibited.

If we view the traditional female role as an ascribed one and the traditional male role as an achieved one, then suicidal behavior should be more common in males, whereas homicidal behavior should be more common in females. Only the first of these predictions can be confirmed. In the United States, males show both more suicidal behavior and more homicidal behavior.

The traditional roles change somewhat during time of war. In times of war, when males are drafted into the armed forces, females take over many of the traditional male roles in society. They thus become more able to achieve a role in the society. Lester (1972) reviewed information on suicide rates during time of war and found some evidence for a relatively higher female suicide rate.

Several studies have looked at the association between the extent to which women are in the labor force and the overall suicide rate of a region. Newman, et al. (1973) found in two U.S. cities (Atlanta and Chicago) that the suicide rate was higher in those census tracts with a higher proportion of females in the labor force. Although Lester (1973) failed to replicate this association using data from Buffalo, Stack (1978) replicated the association using a sample of 45 nations of the world.

The reasons for this association are far from clear, and none of the studies have tried to clarify them. It may be that more married and working females are committing suicide in areas where more females are in the labor force, possibly because of role strain. On the other hand, it may be that the participation of females in the labor force creates additional stress for men (both those in the labor force competing with the females and those married to the working females), thereby increasing their suicide rate. Or it may be that the association is a spurious one, resulting from the importance of some other major sociological variable that is also associated with the percentage of females in the labor force (for example, industrialization).

Cumming, et al. (1975) reported that married women who were employed in British Columbia, Canada, had a lower suicide rate than those who were not employed. They concluded that there was no evidence for the existence of role strain in married working women. Incidentally, the suicide rates for single, widowed, and divorced women who were employed were also lower than those of the unemployed. Thus, employment is associated with a lowered suicide rate for all women, regardless of marital status.

Future studies are necessary to explore why geographic regions with many working females have a higher suicide rate.

FINAL COMMENTS

At a macroscopic level of analysis, there is some evidence for a relationship between sex roles and suicide. The effects of marital status on the suicide rates in males and females, the prediction by college students of suicide in masculine and feminine males and females, the sex difference in suicidal behavior, and the theoretical ideas of Henry and Short on ascribed versus achieved status all lend support to the notion that sex roles are related to suicidal behavior.

Sex roles also involve particular kinds of relationships between men and women. Two problems confront us here. What are the characteristics of the relationships between men and women, for example, between husbands and wives? What are the characteristics of the interpersonal relationships of those prone to suicide? Neither of these questions is easily answered.

Virtually no research has been conducted on the interpersonal relationships of those who complete suicide. Their death makes collection of data difficult. Interviews with the friends and relatives of the deceased person (often called psychological autopsies) yield some information, but it is generally unreliable. Informants often have a distorted perception of the deceased's behavior and personality, and their reports are not an adequate substitute for objective psychological test scores or the observations of expert clinicians. Thus, most of the information on the interpersonal relationships of suicidal individuals has been collected from studies of those who attempt suicide, and many suicidologists have argued that the study of attempted suicide can tell us little that is relevant to completed suicides (Lester, 1972).

At a microscopic level of analysis, where we explore the relationship between actual behavioral roles and the frequency and kind of suicidal behavior in individual people, we find little systematic research. It is, of course, easier to study distal variables (such as marital status) than to study proximal variables (such as the nature of an individual's role). The data are more readily available and distal variables are operationally defined more easily than proximal variables.

The result is that we have some interesting possibilities as to how and why sex roles might be related to suicidal behavior. But we have little concrete evidence from studies of individuals that sex roles *per se* are (or are not) related to suicidal behavior.

REFERENCES

Barno, A.: Criminal abortion deaths, illegitimate pregnancy deaths and suicides in pregnancy. *American Journal of Obstetrics and Gynecology*, 98: 356-367, 1967.

Beck, A. T., Lester, D., and Kovacs, M.: Attempted suicide by males and females. *Psychological Reports*, 33: 965-966, 1973.

Bock, E. W., and Webber, I. L.: Suicide among the elderly. *Journal of Marriage and the Family*, 34: 24-31, 1972.

Burvill, P.: Recent decreased ratio of male/female suicide rates. *International Journal of Social Psychiatry*, 18: 137-139, 1972.

Cumming, E., Lazer, C., and Chisholm, L.: Suicide as an index of role strain among employed and not employed married women in British Columbia. *Canadian Review of Sociology and Anthropology*, 12: 462-470, 1975.

Davis, F.: Sex differences in suicide and attempted suicide. *Diseases of the Nervous System*, 29: 193-194, 1968.

de Graaf, A. C., and Kruyt, C. S.: Some results of the response to a national survey of suicide and attempted suicide in the Netherlands. In *Suicide and attempted suicide in young people*. Copenhagen: World Health Organization, 1976.

Diggory, J. C., and Rothman, D.: Values destroyed by death. *Journal of Abnormal and Social Psychology*, 63: 205-210, 1961.

Durkheim, E.: *Suicide*. New York: Free Press, 1951.

Farberow, N. L.: Self-destruction and identity. *Humanitas*, 6: 45-68, 1970.

Farberow, N. L., and Shneidman, E. S.: *The cry for help*. New York: McGraw-Hill, 1961.

Gibbs, J., and Martin, W.: *Status integration and suicide*. Eugene: University of Oregon Press, 1964.

Gove, W.: Sex, marital status and suicide. *Journal of Health and Social Behavior*, 13: 204-213, 1972.

Gove, W.: Sex differences in the epidemiology of mental disorder. In E. S. Gomberg and V. Franks (Eds.), *Gender and disordered behavior.* New York: Brunner/Mazel, 1979. Pp. 23-68.

Hattem, J. V.: Precipitating role of discordant interpersonal relationships in suicidal behavior. *Dissertation Abstracts,* 25: 1335-1336, 1964.

Henry, A., and Short, J.: *Suicide and homicide.* New York: Free Press, 1954.

Herman, J.: Women, divorce and suicide. *Journal of Divorce,* 1: 107-117, 1977.

Kane, F., Daly, R., Wallach, M., and Keeler, M.: Amelioration of premenstrual mood disturbance with a progestational agent. *Diseases of the Nervous System,* 27: 339-342, 1966.

Kessler, R. C., and McRae, J.: Trends in the relationship between sex and attempted suicide. *Journal of Health and Social Behavior,* 24: 98-110, 1983.

Lemkau, P., Tietze, C., and Cooper, M.: Mental hygiene problems in an urban district. *Mental Hygiene,* 26: 100-119, 1942.

Lester, D. Suicidal behavior in men and women. *Mental Hygiene,* 53: 340-345, 1969a.

Lester, D.: The antisuicide pill. *Journal of the American Medical Association,* 208: 1908, 1969b.

Lester, D.: Suicide, sex and mental disorder. *Psychological Reports,* 27: 61-62, 1970.

Lester, D.: *Why people kill themselves.* Springfield, Ill.: Charles C Thomas, 1972.

Lester, D.: Completed suicide and females in the labor force. *Psychological Reports,* 32: 730, 1973.

Lester, D.: Sex differences in suicidal behavior. In E. S. Gomberg and V. Franks (Eds.), *Gender and disordered behavior.* New York: Brunner/Mazel, 1979. Pp. 287-300.

Lester, D.: Suicide. In C. S. Widom (Ed.) *Sex roles and psychopathology.* New York: Plenum, 1984, pp. 145-156.

Linehan, M.: Suicide and attempted suicide. *Perceptual and Motor Skills,* 37: 31-34, 1973.

Marks, A., and Stokes, C.: Socialization, firearms, and suicide. *Social Problems,* 23: 622-629, 1976.

Metropolitan Life: Recent trends in suicide. *Statistical Bulletin,* 57(May), 5-7, 1976.

Newman, J., Whittemore, K., and Newman, H.: Women in the labor force and suicide. *Social Problems,* 21: 220-230, 1973.

Ross, M.: Suicide among physicians. *Diseases of the Nervous System,* 34: 145-150, 1973.

Roth, W. F., and Luton, F. H.: The mental health program in Tennessee. *American Journal of Psychiatry,* 99: 662-675, 1943.

Stack, S.: Suicide. *Social Forces,* 57: 644-653, 1978.

Stewart, A., and Winter, D.: The nature and causes of female suppression. *Signs,* 2: 531-553, 1977.

Vessey, M., McPherson, K., Lawless, M., and Yeates, D.: Oral contraception and serious psychiatric illness. *British Journal of Psychiatry,* 146: 45-49, 1985.

Whitlock, F., and Edwards, J.: Pregnancy and attempted suicide. *Comprehensive Psychiatry,* 9: 1-12, 1968.

Wold, C.: Subgroupings of suicidal people. *Omega,* 2: 19-29, 1971.

Yap, P.: Suicide in Hong Kong. *Journal of Mental Science,* 104: 266-301, 1958.

CHAPTER 2

AN INTERNATIONAL PERSPECTIVE
ON FEMALE SUICIDE

DAVID LESTER

SUICIDE RATES vary greatly from nation to nation, and the female suicide rate relative to the male suicide rate varies greatly too. I have calculated suicide rates for males and females for nations of the world for the period 1979-1981 and the increase in the suicide rates from 1970 to 1980. The data are shown in Table 1.

Table 1

SUICIDE RATES FOR MALES AND FEMALES
FOR NATIONS OF THE WORLD FOR 1979-1981

	suicide rates		male/ female ratio	percent change since 1970	
	male	female		male	female
From WHO Publications					
Argentina	9.7	4.3	2.3	−36.6	−10.4
Australia	16.6	5.9	2.8	−2.9	−28.0
Austria	38.3	14.9	2.6	+16.8	+3.5
Barbados	2.6	0.5	5.2	−18.7	−37.5
Belgium	28.2	15.0	1.9	+30.6	+48.5
Bulgaria	19.4	8.3	2.3	+19.8	+9.2
Canada	21.3	6.9	3.1	+30.7	+9.5
Chile	9.3	1.8	5.2	−7.0	−28.0
Costa Rica	7.0	1.7	4.1	+48.9	+183.3
Czechoslovakia	30.3	9.9	3.1	−15.8	−23.8
Denmark	37.3	21.1	1.8	+30.9	+29.4
Ecuador	3.5	2.1	1.7	+2.9	+90.9

Table 1 (continued)

	suicide rates		male/female ratio	percent change since 1970	
	male	female		male	female
From WHO Publications					
El Salvador	14.7	4.6	3.2	+10.5	+142.1
Finland	40.4	10.0	4.0	+13.5	+5.3
France	27.9	10.9	2.6	+21.8	+28.2
Germany, West	29.0	14.4	2.0	+4.3	−3.4
Greece	4.4	2.0	2.2	−6.4	0.0
Guatemala	1.8	0.2	9.0	−66.0	−85.7
Hong Kong	13.5	11.1	1.2	+15.4	+18.1
Hungary	63.9	27.3	2.3	+26.8	+37.2
Iceland	15.1	5.3	2.8	+45.0	+32.5
Ireland	8.7	3.7	2.4	+171.9	+270.0
Israel	7.8	4.1	1.9	+4.0	−26.8
Italy	9.9	4.3	2.3	+23.7	+22.9
Japan	22.2	13.0	1.7	+29.8	−0.8
Luxembourg	23.4	10.0	2.3	+5.9	+40.8
Malta	0.0	0.0	—	−100.0	—
Mauritius	5.8	2.1	2.8	+61.1	+110.0
Mexico	2.6	0.7	3.7	+85.7	+133.3
Netherlands	12.3	8.1	1.5	+28.1	+30.6
New Zealand	14.5	5.9	2.5	+20.8	−10.6
Norway	18.2	6.7	2.7	+46.8	+63.4
Panama	3.3	0.6	5.5	−31.2	−25.0
Paraguay	3.0	2.4	1.2	+76.5	+71.4
Poland	21.8	4.0	5.4	+14.7	−2.4
Portugal	12.5	4.5	2.8	−3.1	+32.4
Puerto Rico	14.6	2.7	5.4	−2.7	−44.9
Singapore	10.8	8.9	1.2	−4.4	+11.2
Spain	6.5	2.1	3.1	−1.5	0.0
Sri Lanka	37.7	19.7	1.9	+50.2	+80.7
Sweden	26.8	11.6	2.3	−11.6	−8.7
Switzerland	34.9	15.0	2.3	+32.7	+44.2
Thailand	7.4	6.9	1.1	+68.2	+109.1
UK: England & Wales	11.0	6.6	1.7	+11.1	−2.9
Northern Ireland	7.1	3.1	2.3	+29.1	−11.4
Scotland	12.7	7.1	1.8	+41.1	+24.6
USA	18.6	5.7	3.3	+12.7	−12.3
Venezuela	7.6	1.9	4.0	−20.0	−53.7
Yugoslavia	21.0	8.8	2.4	+3.4	+15.8
From WHO (with data missing for 1970)					
Bahamas	1.0	0.0	—		
Belize	1.3	0.0	—		

Table 1 (continued)

	suicide rates		male/ female ratio	percent change since 1970	
	male	female		male	female
From WHO Publications					
Brazil	4.7	2.1	2.2		
Cape Verde	4.4	0.6	7.3		
Cayman Islands	12.3	0.0	—		
Dominica	0.0	0.0	—		
Egypt	0.01	0.0(5)	2.0		
Jordan	0.0	0.0	—		
Kuwait	0.9	0.5	1.8		
Martinique	20.0	4.4	4.5		
Montserrat	0.0	0.0	—		
Netherlands Antilles	3.2	0.8	4.0		
Papua-New Guinea	0.1	0.2	0.5		
St Kitts & Nevis	1.7	0.0	—		
St Lucia	1.7	0.0	—		
St Vincent & Grenadines	1.9	0.0	—		
Seychelles	3.1	3.1	1.0		
Suriname	17.8	10.8	1.6		
Syria	0.6	0.1	6.0		
From Other Data Sources					
Taiwan	11.1	8.6	1.3		
India	6.9	5.1	1.4		

Lester (1982) examined a similar but smaller set of data for the year 1975. Lester concluded that Asian nations had proportionately more female suicides. The female/male ratio was significantly higher in Asia (average 0.74) than in Europe (0.45) and in South America & Central America/Caribbean nations (0.34).

Lester also looked at the distribution of suicide rates by age for each sex in each nation as a function of the level of economic development of each nation (defined as the gross national product per capita). For males, in nations at all levels of economic development, suicide rates rose with age. However, for females, the peak age for suicide rose from 55-64 to 75+ as the level of economic development of the nations increased, until the least developed group of nations where the peak dropped to 15-24.

Correlates of Female Suicide Rates

Several research studies have explored correlates of the female suicide rate in nations of the world and of the female/male ratio.

In a study of eighteen industrialized nations, Lester (1974) found that male and female suicide rates were strongly related. Lester looked at the *male/female* suicide rate ratio and found that it was positively associated with the number of psychiatric patients per capita in the nations, the dependency ratio for the elderly (that is the proportion of the population that is old), and the summer humidity, and negatively with the rate of deaths from ulcers and the mean annual temperature. Lester (1982) studied a less restricted sample of nations and found that the female/male ratio was not related to the gross national product per capita.

Stewart and Winter (1977) derived indices of female suppression in nations of the world and reported scores for two components: social-educational equality and economic equality. (They also derived a component that they labelled impulse control.) The male-minus-female suicide rate was not associated with either measure of equality (but was positively associated with the component of impulse control.[1]

Stack has carried several studies of suicide rates in nations of the world. Stack (1981) studied the association between religion and suicide rates. He found that the proportion of Roman Catholics in a nation was not related to either the male or the female suicide rates, though divorce rates correlated with both rates. Stack (1983) assessed religiosity in nations of the world by measuring the percentage of books published in each nation that were religious. Stack found that only female suicide rates correlated with this measure of religiosity (negatively). Stack felt that this result made sense since religious commitment is probably stronger for women than for men. (Industrialization as measured by the gross national product per capita and gender-equality as measured by Stewart and Winter correlated similarly with both male and female suicide rates.)

An Analysis in Industrialized Nations

For the present chapter, I took Lynn's sample of eighteen industrialized nations and examined correlates of the female suicide rate for 1970.

The eighteen nation sample includes Australia, Austria, Belgium, Canada, Denmark, Finland, France, Ireland, Italy, Japan, the Netherlands, New Zealand, Norway, Sweden, Switzerland, the United Kingdom, the USA and West Germany.

---

1. Impulse control was comprised of a higher divorce rate, higher infant mortality, earlier marriage, lower life expectancy, and fewer illegitimate births.

The societal variables used in the analysis included national measures of anxiety and extraversion (Lynn, 1982), two measures of female inequality (Stewart and Winter, 1977), the quality of life (Estes, 1984), participation of females in the labor force, population density, percent of the population 0-14 and over 65, percent of population living in urban areas, and the birth rate (World Bank, 1976), government sanctions and the percentage of Roman Catholics (Taylor and Hudson, 1972), the divorce rate and the long-term immigration rate from the United Nations annual *Demographic Yearbooks,* the gross national product per capita from the US Census Bureau's *Statistical Abstract of the United States, 1971,* and the percentage of books produced that are religious from Stack (1983). The 1970 suicide rates were obtained from a data set compiled by the author.

The societal variables were factor-analyzed (using SPSSX Factor, with a principal components extraction and a varimax rotation) and five factors identified. These were then correlated with the male suicide rate, the female suicide rate and the ratio of the female/male rates. The results are shown in Table 2.

Table 2

SOCIETAL CORRELATES OF FEMALE SUICIDE RATES
IN INDUSTRIALIZED NATIONS

	Factor #				
	I	II	III	IV	V
anxiety	20	14	59*	56*	06
extraversion	82*	03	15	−39	12
quality of life	−71*	47	−30	−18	−04
gnp/capita	86*	19	−10	−17	−25
birth rate	−10	−88*	−28	−06	−02
% children	09	−84*	−34	−22	15
% elderly	08	86*	−17	14	20
pop. density	−20	19	05	78*	−23
% urban pop.	17	−24	−26	08	−80*
% females in labor force	25	32	83*	−12	−13
gov. sanctions	73*	01	33	24	24
% Roman Catholics	10	−06	−27	62*	58*
divorce rate	81*	10	25	−36	−26
% religious books	02	−10	−28	−02	88*
female equality:					
social/educational	24	−13	−13	−79*	−08
economic	18	−01	90*	12	−05

Table 2 (continued)

suicide rates:	Factor #				
	I	II	III	IV	V
male	0.15	0.60*	0.51*	−0.13	−0.01
female	0.08	0.57*	0.48*	0.06	−0.33
female/male	−0.13	0.04	0.20	0.32	−0.74*

The loadings are shown without the decimal place. For example, 0.20 is written as 20.

* a high loading, or a statistically significant correlation

It can be seen that both the male and female suicide rates correlated with the age-composition factor and the participation of females in the labor force factor. The ratio of the female/male rates was correlated with the religion/urbanization factor.

Discussion

It has been shown in this chapter that the female suicide rate relative to the male suicide rate varies greatly from nation to nation. Females complete suicide at a relatively higher rate in Asia and at a lower rate in South and Central America.

For industrialized nations, it has been shown that both male and female suicide rates have similar social correlates (including the age composition in the nation and the participation of females in the labor force). The female suicide rate relative to the male suicide rate was associated only with the religiosity/urbanization factor.

Much more research needs to be conducted on the differential correlates of the female suicide rate in nations of the world, and it hoped that this chapter will stimulate such research.

REFERENCES

Estes, R. J.: *The social progress of nations.* New York: Praeger, 1984.

Lester, D.: A cross-national study of suicide and homicide. *Behavior Science Research,* 9: 307-318, 1974.

Lester, D.: The distribution of sex and age among completed suicides. *International Journal of Social Psychiatry,* 28: 256-260, 1982.

Lynn, R.: National differences in anxiety and extroversion. *Progress in Experimental Personality Research,* 11: 213-258, 1982.

Stack, S.: Suicide and religion. *Sociological Focus,* 14: 207-220, 1981.

Stack, S.: The effect of religious commitment of suicide. *Journal of Health & Social Behavior,* 24: 362-374, 1983.

Stewart, A. J., & Winter, D. G.: The nature and causes of female suppression. *Signs,* 2: 531-553, 1977.

Taylor, C. L., & Hudson, M. C.: *World handbook of political and social indicators.* New Haven: Yale University Press, 1972.

World Bank: *World Tables, 1976.* Baltimore: Johns Hopkins University Press, 1976.

CHAPTER 3

THE SUICIDE RATES
OF WOMEN IN AMERICA

DAVID LESTER

THE SUICIDE rates of women vary greatly across America. For example, as can be seen in Table 1, both male and female suicide rates were highest in Nevada in 1980 and lowest in New Jersey.

Table 1

SUICIDE RATES FOR MALES AND FEMALES FOR THE USA IN 1980

| | suicide rate | | male/female |
	male	female	ratio
AL	19.3	3.7	5.22
AZ	26.3	7.8	3.37
AR	18.5	5.2	3.56
CA	21.4	7.7	2.78
CO	25.2	7.4	3.41
CT	14.2	4.0	3.55
DE	17.8	6.5	2.74
FL	23.0	8.4	2.74
GA	19.9	5.8	3.43
ID	21.7	4.7	4.62
IL	15.1	3.9	3.87
IN	17.5	3.8	4.61
IA	19.0	3.5	5.43
KS	16.6	5.5	3.02
KY	20.7	5.3	3.91
LA	19.8	5.0	3.96
ME	20.3	5.2	3.90

Table 1 (continued)

	suicide rate		male/female
	male	female	ratio
MD	17.0	4.9	3.47
MA	12.9	4.0	3.22
MI	18.0	5.3	3.40
MN	17.0	4.9	3.47
MS	14.9	3.8	3.92
MO	19.0	5.3	3.58
MT	23.2	5.8	4.00
NE	17.0	3.5	4.86
NV	30.1	15.4	1.95
NH	17.4	4.9	3.55
NJ	12.7	2.5	5.08
NM	28.5	6.7	4.25
NY	14.4	5.1	2.82
NC	17.4	5.3	3.28
ND	18.0	4.0	4.50
OH	18.7	5.6	3.34
OK	19.9	6.5	3.06
OR	23.7	5.8	4.09
PA	18.1	4.7	3.85
RI	17.1	5.8	2.95
SC	15.2	4.2	3.62
SD	22.0	3.7	5.95
TN	19.0	5.9	3.22
TX	19.3	5.5	3.51
UT	19.3	7.2	2.68
VT	23.3	6.5	3.58
VA	21.6	5.5	3.93
WA	20.5	6.2	3.31
WV	20.6	4.8	4.29
WI	18.6	5.1	3.65
WY	24.1	7.4	3.26

However, the ratio of the male suicide rate to the female suicide rate ranged from 1.95 in Nevada to 5.95 in South Dakota. In this chapter we will explore which sociological variables are associated with the female suicide rate and the male-to-female suicide rate ratio and which variables best predict these indices of female self-destructive behavior.

Correlates of the Female Suicide Rate

Many regional studies of suicide rates in America have been reported, using a variety of sociological variables (for example, Lester,

1987; Stack, 1980). In some regional studies, primarily of the census tracts in single cities, the male and female suicide rates have been found to have different correlates. For example, Diggory and Lester (1976) studied the census tracts in Buffalo and reported that the male suicide rate was associated with the incidence of the widowed and divorced and the incidence of unemployed males. The female suicide, in contrast, was associated with the median family income.

For this chapter, a wide selection of sociological variables was made from those which have been used in previous research, and all of them explored for their association with male and female suicide rates. The sociological variables used are listed in Table 2.

Table 2

CORRELATES OF THE MALE AND FEMALE SUICIDE RATES IN 1980

	suicide rate male	suicide rate female	female suicide rate controlling for the male rate	male/ female suicide rate
divorce rate	0.69*	0.80*	0.60*	−0.32*
interstate migration	0.74*	0.71*	0.38*	−0.28*
% black	−0.34*	−0.16	0.13	−0.07
church attendance	−0.45*	−0.48*	−0.26*	0.30*
% Roman Catholic	−0.13	0.01	0.16	−0.13
birth rate	0.36*	0.18	−0.13	0.06
% voting for Reagan	0.33*	0.27*	0.04	0.05
% married women working:				
full-time	0.08	0.23	0.24*	−0.17
part-time	−0.17	−0.16	−0.05	0.08
% urban population	−0.04	0.32*	0.50*	−0.45*
% separated	−0.24	0.04	0.32*	−0.28*
% divorced	0.71*	0.82*	0.63*	−0.42*
homicide rate	0.17	0.32*	0.30*	−0.28*
crime rate	0.31*	0.61*	0.58*	−0.56*
unemployment rate	−0.09	−0.11	−0.07	0.05
% elderly	−0.28*	−0.30*	−0.15	0.20
male unemployment rate	−0.07	−0.10	−0.07	0.05
females in labor force	0.01	0.17	0.25*	−0.15
east-west	0.60*	0.44*	0.01	−0.03
north-south	−0.07	−0.13	−0.11	0.13
fluoridated water	−0.24*	−0.33*	−0.24	0.14

Table 2 (continued)

	suicide rate		female suicide rate controlling for the male rate	male/ female suicide rate
	male	female		
median family income	−0.17	0.10	0.33*	−0.25*
per capita income	−0.12	0.19	0.40*	−0.31*
population	−0.24*	−0.03	0.22	−0.23
population density	−0.56*	−0.26	0.24	−0.08
strictness of state handgun control laws	−0.58*	−0.44*	−0.03	0.12
southerness	0.21	0.16	0.01	−0.10
MS magazine subscriptions	0.07	0.12	0.11	−0.17

*significant at p < 0.05 or better

The product-moment correlations of these sociological variables with the male and female suicide rates over the continental states in 1980 are shown in Table 2.

It can be seen that both male and female suicide rates were associated with similar variables: the divorce rate, interstate migration, church attendance, the percent voting for Reagan as President, the incidence of divorced people, the crime rate, the percent of elderly, East-West, the extent of fluoridated drinking water, and the strictness of state handgun control laws.

However, the female suicide rate was also associated with the percent of the population that was urban and the homicide rate. (The male suicide rate was also associated with the percent black, the population of the state and the population density.)

To see what sociological variables were especially relevant to the female suicide, given that the overall suicide rate varies greatly over the states, partial correlation coefficients were calculated between the sociological variables and the female suicide rate controlling for the male suicide rate. These correlations are shown in Table 2.

It can be seen that the female suicide rate was associated with the divorce rate, the rate of interstate migration, church attendance, the involvement of women in the labor force and the percentage of married women working full-time, urbanization, the percentage of people separated and divorced, the homicide and crime rates, the median family income and the per capita income.

However, the results of a factor analysis (see Table 3) showed that the male and female suicide rates were loaded on the same factor along with the divorce rate, church attendance, the percentage of divorced people,

East-West, population density, the strictness of the state handgun control law, and the crime rate. This seems to reflect an East-West variation in attitudes and behaviors, with both the male and female suicide rates being higher in the West.

Table 3

THE RESULTS OF THE FACTOR ANALYSIS
OF THE VARIABLES

	Factor I	Factor II
divorce rate	0.86*	0.03
interstate migration	0.78	−0.03
% black	−0.27	0.01
church attendance	−0.69*	−0.04
% Roman Catholic	−0.07	0.55*
% voting for Reagan	0.19	0.00
% married women working		
full-time	0.22	−0.19
part-time	−0.21	0.17
% urban population	0.05	0.95*
% separated	−0.15	0.35
% divorced	0.92*	0.20
birth rate	0.11	−0.18
unemployment rate	−0.03	−0.02
male unemployment rate	−0.03	0.03
% elderly	−0.20	−0.12
females in the labor force	0.11	0.21
east-west	0.51*	0.06
% fluoridated water	−0.29	0.05
median family income	−0.04	0.76*
per capita income	0.07	0.81*
population	−0.18	0.62*
population density	−0.45*	0.53*
strictness of state handgun control law	−0.61*	0.25
MS Magazine subscriptions	0.14	0.45*
southerness	0.22	−0.17
south-north	−0.06	−0.06
crime rate	0.48*	0.75*
homicide rate	0.23	0.26
female suicide rate	0.84*	0.28
male suicide rate	0.84*	−0.13
male/female suicide rate ratio	−0.40	−0.49*

*indicates a high loading of the variable on the Factor (PC extraction, varimax rotation, using SPSSX)

Multiple regressions have been very popular in the last decade, although I find them inappropriate for understanding a phenomenon. Multiple regression identifies the best predictors of a target variable and selects arbitarily the variables with highest correlation with the target variable despite the fact that the strength of the associations of several predictor variables with the target variable may not differ significantly. Factor analysis avoids this conceptual error.

However, for readers who prefer multiple regression, the results of backward multiple regressions (using SPSSX) are shown in Table 4. It can be seen that, on the whole, the predictors of the male and the female suicide rates are different. Only interstate migration appeared in both sets of predictors.

Table 4

RESULTS OF THE MULTIPLE REGRESSIONS

	beta coefficient	p
Female Suicide Rate		
male unemployment rate	0.70	0.02
church attendance	0.29	0.01
% separated	0.34	0.0003
interstate migration	0.36	0.006
% divorced	0.81	<0.0001
unemployment rate	−0.70	0.02
Male Suicide Rate		
homicide rate	0.58	<0.0001
birth rate	−0.33	0.0007
median family income	−0.42	0.0004
females in labor force	0.33	0.02
% elderly	−0.34	0.0006
population density	−0.36	0.0002
interstate migration	0.59	<0.0001
% black	−0.36	0.005
% married women working full-time	−0.57	0.0003
Male/Female Suicide Rate Ratio		
birth rate	−0.44	0.02
church attendance	−0.51	0.02
east-west	0.88	0.0003
crime rate	−0.78	0.0001
south-north	−0.79	0.02
divorce rate	0.87	0.02
% divorced	−1.45	0.003
% married women working part-time	0.99	0.007
unemployment rate	0.37	0.01

The Male/Female Suicide Rate Ratio

The correlations of the male/female suicide rates with the sociological variables are shown in Table 2. The male/female suicide rate ratio was positively associated with church attendance and negatively associated with the divorce rate, interstate migration, urbanization, the percentage of people separated and divorced, the homicide and crime rates, the median family income and the per capita income.

On the factor analysis, the male/female suicide rate ratio was loaded on the same factor as the percentage of Roman Catholics, urbanization, the median family income and the per capita income, the population and population density, subscriptions to MS Magazine, and the crime rate. The results of the multiple regression are shown in Table 4.

An Alternative Conceptualization of the Results

A different way of presenting the results that is perhaps clearer is shown in Table 5. All of the sociological variables were factor analyzed (using SPSSX's principal components analysis with a varimax rotation), and seven factors identified. Then the seven factors scores were correlated with the male and female suicide rates (and homicide rates for comparison purposes).

Table 5

THE RESULTS OF A FACTOR ANALYSIS OF THE SOCIAL INDICATORS
AND THE CORRELATIONS OF THESE FACTORS
WITH SUICIDE RATES AND HOMICIDE RATES

Social Indicator	Factor						
	I	II	III	IV	V	VI	VII
divorce rate	−0.18	0.02	0.85*	0.23	−0.08	0.05	−0.10
interstate migration	0.07	−0.04	0.74*	0.31	−0.37	0.10	−0.30
percent black	−0.79*	0.03	−0.21	−0.34	0.04	0.35	−0.04
church attendance	0.07	−0.15	−0.77*	0.25	−0.23	−0.23	−0.01
% Roman Catholic	0.56*	0.51*	−0.08	−0.36	0.04	−0.21	−0.21
% vote for Reagan	0.10	0.02	0.12	0.80*	−0.33	−0.06	−0.13
% married women							
full-time work	−0.49*	−0.19	0.26	−0.14	−0.52*	0.49*	0.17
part-time work	0.92*	0.12	−0.23	0.06	−0.16	0.05	−0.01
% urban population	−0.02	0.95*	0.04	0.09	−0.04	−0.03	−0.06
% separated	−0.51*	0.36	−0.10	−0.52	0.02	0.43*	−0.18
% divorced	−0.01	0.19	0.92*	0.17	0.07	0.07	−0.02
birth rate	−0.08	−0.17	0.02	0.89*	−0.07	0.22	−0.21
unemployment rate	−0.11	−0.01	0.02	−0.17	0.94*	0.07	0.02
% over 65 years	0.06	−0.11	−0.19	−0.32	−0.06	−0.80*	0.12
females in labor force	0.51*	0.17	0.12	−0.05	−0.54*	0.48*	0.19

Table 5 (continued)

Social Indicator	I	II	III	Factor IV	V	VI	VII
east-west	0.07	0.09	0.47*	0.73*	0.02	0.10	0.03
north-south	0.91*	−0.11	−0.06	0.04	0.12	0.09	0.07
fluoride in water	0.04	0.06	−0.27	−0.15	0.06	−0.06	0.82*
median family income	0.46*	0.75*	−0.01	−0.01	0.02	0.28	0.10
per capita income	0.41*	0.79*	0.12	−0.13	−0.12	0.10	0.15
population	−0.26	0.64*	−0.14	−0.10	0.28	−0.07	0.27
population density	0.15	0.52*	−0.41*	−0.50*	−0.01	−0.09	−0.25
gun control laws	0.07	0.25	−0.57*	−0.24	0.19	0.24	0.14
MS subscriptions	0.76*	0.40*	0.15	−0.26	−0.06	0.10	0.08
southerness	−0.89*	−0.12	0.26	0.02	0.13	0.13	0.11
crime rate	−0.01	0.74*	0.49*	−0.06	0.01	0.12	−0.14
male unemployment rate	0.01	0.04	0.01	−0.11	0.95*	0.01	0.11

Correlation of Factors with Suicide (and Homicide) Rates

	I	II	III	IV	V	VI	VII
Suicide Rate: total	−0.03	0.02	0.82#	0.30#	−0.06	0.01	−0.11
male	0.01	−0.10	0.77#	0.33#	−0.01	−0.05	−0.07
female	−0.10	0.25#	0.77#	0.16	−0.12	0.05	−0.16
male/female	0.14	−0.41#	−0.33#	0.09	0.08	−0.11	0.09
Homicide Rate: total	−0.84#	0.29#	0.25#	−0.06	0.12	0.04	0.04
male	−0.84#	0.29#	0.17	−0.08	0.13	0.01	0.06
female	−0.69#	0.26#	0.45#	−0.04	0.06	0.12	−0.06
male/female	−0.34#	0.05	−0.15	−0.21	0.12	−0.12	0.09

Factor Labels: I southerness
II urban/wealthier
III divorced/mobile
IV west/conservative
V unemployment
VI elderly
VII fluoride in water

*high loading of a variable on a factor

#statistically significant correlation

It can be seen that male and female suicide rates were both correlated with Factor III, tentatively labelled as high rates of divorced and mobile people. Whereas female suicide rates were also correlated with Factor II (urban and wealthy), male suicide rates were correlated with Factor IV (West and conservative). These secondary correlations were much weaker than the correlation of the suicide rates with Factor III.

It can be seen that the correlations of the factor scores with the homicide rates were somewhat different. For homicide rates, Factor I (southerness) was the strongest correlate while Factors II and III were secondary correlates.

Discussion

It can be seen that both male and female suicide rates vary greatly over the states of the continental USA, generally increasing with the incidence of divorced and mobile people. Male suicide rates vary also with longitude and conservatism while female suicide rates vary with urbanization and wealth.

Similarly, the ratio of the male suicide rate to the female suicide rate varies over the states of the USA. The male/female suicide rate ratio was higher in the less urban and wealthy states and in the states with fewer divorced and mobile people.

It is difficult to speculate, even *post hoc,* about the reasons for the different patterns of correlations identified for males and females in this ecological study. Furthermore, since the empirical findings in this chapter are correlational, the results do not provide answers about the *causes* of the differences between male and female suicide rates. However, it is hoped that the study will stimulate hypotheses and further research on the topic.

REFERENCES

Diggory, J. C., & Lester, D.: Suicide rates of men and women. *Omega,* 7: 95-101, 1976.

Lester, D.: Religion, suicide and homicide. *Social Psychiatry,* 22: 99-101, 1987.

Stack, S.: The effects of interstate migration on suicide. *International Journal of Social Psychiatry,* 26: 17-25, 1980.

CHAPTER 4

WOMEN, WORK, AND SUICIDE

BIJOU YANG

T HE FACT THAT economic conditions are related to the incidence
of suicide has long been recognized. Durkheim (1951) predicted
that suicide rates should increase during times of economic changes, regardless of the direction of the economic change. During periods of economic boom or bust, the degree of both social integration and social
regulation is diminished, and this leads to an increased tendency toward
suicide.

Henry and Short (1954) found a negative correlation between the
suicide rate and economic conditions. As the economy contracts, the
suicide rate increases and *pari passu* when the economy expands. Simon
(1968) also noted that the suicide rate decreases as the economy grows.
Suicide rates for both men and women decreased during periods of economic prosperity and increased during periods preceding economic crisis (Araki, et al, 1987).

Unemployment and Suicide

Robin, et al. (1968) reported substantially more unemployment in
males who had completed suicide than in a control group of nonsuicidal
individuals. Tuckman and Youngman (1968) also found that unemployment indicated a greater risk of subsequent completed suicide among attempted suicides.

Whitlock and Schapira (1967) in England and Edwards and Whitlock
(1968) in Australia found that males who had attempted suicide were
more likely to be unemployed than males in the general population. A
correlation over time between the proportion of unemployed and the

35

suicide rate in the United States from 1930 to 1960 showed that the association was positive and strong for white males, especially those aged 45 to 54.

More recently, Platt (1984) has reviewed all of the studies that have been conducted on the relationship between unemployment and both completed and attempted suicide, including the studies mentioned above, and concluded that the evidence consistently supports the existence of the relationship.

At a very general level, suicide rate is related not only to the unemployment rate but also to income. Rushing (1968) looked at the completed suicide rate, the income, and the employment rate for various occupations. For occupations with high unemployment rates, the suicide rate was negatively related to income, whereas for occupations with low unemployment rate, the suicide rate was positively related to income. For occupations with high income, the suicide rate was not related to the unemployment rate, whereas for occupations with low income, the suicide rate was positively related to the unemployment rate.

Occupational Status

Studies have investigated the effects of occupational status upon the suicide rate, but they have generated conflicting results. Kalish (1968) who studied Hawaii and Stengel (1964) who studied England both reported that the completed suicide rate was highest in those with the highest occupational status.

On the other hand, Tuckman, et al. (1964) investigated the relationship between occupational status and the suicide rate of white males in the United States and found a significant negative correlation, indicating that the suicide rate was higher in those with a lower occupational status. Buckle, et al. (1965) compared a sample of attempted suicides in Australia with patients admitted to the same hospital matched for sex and age and found that the attempted suicides were more likely to have unskilled occupations.

Suicide in Particular Professions

Different professions seem to be associated with different degrees of stress, and the suicide rate of these professions varies.

Farber (1968) felt that those who provided nurturance and help to others would have an increased rate of suicide. For example, Maris

(1967) noted that in Cook County, Illinois, the suicide rates of service workers (policemen, barbers, housekeepers, nurses, etc.) were higher than those of craftsmen (carpenters, tailors, etc.) and operators (taxi drivers, assemblers, apprentices, etc.).

Blachly, et al. (1968) noted that although physicians as a whole do not have a suicide rate markedly different from that of the general population, the rates vary within the profession. Pediatricians had the lowest rate while psychiatrists had the highest rate.

Other investigators have reported a high suicide rate for physicians. In California, Rose and Rosow (1973) found a high rate of suicide for physicians, but they also found high rates for chemists, dentists, pharmacists, musicians, and non-medical technicians. The lowest rates were found for college teachers, clergymen, and social workers.

Li (1969) found male chemists to have a suicide rate comparable to that of the general population, but female chemists had an unusually high rate. Zung and Moore (1976) found that crisis intervention volunteers had a higher incidence of suicide attempts than hospital staff members. Mausner and Steppacher (1973) found a lower rate of suicide than expected for male psychologists but a higher rate than expected for female psychologists.

Heiman (1975) found a higher suicide rate for police officers in New York City than for white urban males in general. Lester (1978) reviewed all of the available data and concluded that American police officers do indeed kill themselves at a higher rate than men in other occupations.

Women Professionals

Men kill themselves at a higher rate than do women. Studies of suicide in the United States have indicated that the completed suicide rate is higher for men than for women (see Chapter 1). However, in certain professions, females appear to have a higher suicide rate than their male counterparts.

Female chemists were found by Li (1969) to have a higher rate of suicide than male chemists. Mausner and Steppacher (1973) reported a higher rate of suicide than expected for female psychologists. Some other recent studies (Craig and Pitts, 1968; Steppacher and Mausner, 1974; Pitts et al., 1979) have uncovered what appears to be very high rates of suicide among female physicians in the United States.

In a study that examined the factors behind the high rate of suicide of female physicians, Carlson and Miller (1981) proposed that those at greater risk for depressive disorder (thereby at a higher risk of suicide) are in their 20s, 30s, and 40s. These are periods in life when the psychosocial stressors involved with medical training, career choice, and role conflicts are maximal. Those without a support system of colleagues and family are at even higher risk. The authors hypothesized that not only do female physicians have the intelligence and education to plan a suicide, but they also have the knowledge and means available to successfully kill themselves before the impulse subsides, leaving little margin for error or change of mind. The same hypothesis may apply also to other female professionals, such as female psychologists and chemists.

Women and Employment

What is the impact for women of employment in general on their incidence of suicide? The question can be answered at two levels. One relates the employment of women to their mental health in general. The other examines the impact on their suicidal behavior.

Regarding the first issue, it has been found that work for women leads to reduced contact with their spouse and children (Staines and Pleck, 1983), reduced affection from their spouse and less harmony (Geeken and Gove, 1983), and more guilt (Mortimer and London, 1984). Compared with other groups, married women with full-time jobs experience the highest tension; housewives show the least; married women working part-time are in between (Michelson, 1985).

Baruch, et al. (1987), after reviewing the benefits and the costs of the employment of women, concluded that work is not always beneficial to women. The jobs most likely to involve stressors that impair health are those that demand a great deal but permit very little autonomy. Such jobs are typically low-level and low-paying ones.

However, some studies draw very different conclusions. A variety of well-controlled studies show significant mental and physical health differences that favor employed women over non-employed women (Merikangas, 1985; Verbrugge, 1982; Waldron and Herold, 1984).

These are studies which related the employment of women and their general mental health. In contrast, some research has investigated the incidence of women's *suicide* to employment. For example, Steffensmeier (1984) suggested that the increase in female suicide rates during the 1960s and the subsequent stability of female rates during the 1970s might be related to changes over time in the degree of social integration and the role conflict of working women, responses to broad societal changes occuring during the 1960s, and to the development of ideological support for an acceptance of role changes in the sexual, marital, and economic realms.

It can be seen that these issues have not yet received much attention from social science researchers.

Female in Labor Force

It has been argued that the participation of females in labor force is a source of conflict (Miley and Micklin, 1972; Newman, et al., 1973). Stack (1978) has suggested that this conflict may result in higher rates of suicide among married women due to the role conflict created between household and working responsibilities.

Theoretically, the participation of females in the labor force fits best with the theory of status integration proposed by Gibbs and Martin (1964). Gibbs and Martin felt that the degree to which the different statuses held by people in a society were integrated (and free from conflict) would be related to the suicide rate. Stack (1978) used the participation of females in the labor force as an index of status integration. Stack argued that, the more females participate in the labor force, the lower the status integration of the society and thus the higher the suicide rate.

Three studies on this topic have focused on census tracts within major American cities. Newman, et al. (1973) found that census tracts with a higher rate of participation of females in the labor force had higher overall suicide rates in both Atlanta and Chicago. However, Lester (1973) failed to find any association in Buffalo for the overall suicide rate, and Diggory and Lester (1976) failed to find any association for female suicide rate. But, in a study of 45 nations, Stack (1978) found a positive association between the participation of females in the labor force and the overall suicide rate, even after controlling for the variables of industrialization and the rate of economic growth.

Incidentally, Davis (1981) reported a time-series analysis for the United States as a whole for 1950 to 1969 and found that total female participation in the labor force and the participation of married women were positively associated with the female suicide rate but not with the male suicide rate.

Yeh and Lester (1988) conducted a regional study of the continental states of the USA and identified the divorce rate, the degree of urbanization, and the amount of interstate migration as predictors of suicide rates. The rate of married women working full time did not have a significant effect on the female suicide rate.

Conclusions

The incidence of suicide appears to be related to some extent to economic conditions. Some theorists believe that, as the economy grows, the suicide rate decreases. Others suggest that, regardless of economic boom or bust, suicide rates increase during any economic change.

The suicide rate is found to be higher in the unemployed than in the employed. Among the employed, the suicide rate varies among different professional groups. The suicide rate seems higher in those of service workers than those of craftsmen and of operators. A higher rate of suicide is also found in psychiatrists and other physicians, female chemists, crisis intervention volunteers, police officers, dentists, pharmacists, musicians, and non-medical technicians.

In certain professions, female professionals have a higher suicide rate than their male counterparts; in particular, female chemists, psychologists, and physicians. For female physicians the reason appears to be related to the fact that the risk of depressive disorder is greater for women in their 20s, 30s, and 40s. These are periods when the psychosocial stressors involved in their life are maximal. In addition, these women have the intelligence, education and knowledge to plan a suicide successfully. The same explanation may apply to other female professional groups.

In general, the participation of females in the labor force has been found to be positively related to the suicide rate, perhaps because this female participation increases role conflict.

REFERENCES

Araki, S., and Murata, K.: Suicide in Japan: socioeconomic effects on its secular and seasonal trends. *Suicide & Life-Threatening Behavior,* 17: 64-71, 1987.

Baruch, G. K., Biener, L., and Barnett, R. C.: Women and gender in research on work and family stress. *American Psychologist,* 42: 130-136, 1987.

Blachly, P. H., Disher, W., and Roduner, G.: Suicide by physicians. *Bulletin of Suicidology,* December: 1-18, 1968.

Buckle, R. C., Linane, J., and McConaghy, N.: Attempted suicides presenting at the Alfred Hospital, Melbourne. *Medical Journal of Australia,* 1: 754-758, 1965.

Carlson, G. A., and Miller, D. C.: Suicide, affective disorder, and women physicians. *American Journal of Psychiatry,* 138: 1330-1335, 1981.

Craig, A. G., and Pitts, F. N.: Suicide by physicians. *Diseases of the Nervous System,* 29: 763-772, 1968.

Davis, R.: Female labor force participation, status intergration and suicide, 1950-1969. *Suicide & Life-Threatening Behavior,* 11: 111-123, 1981.

Diggory, J. D., and Lester, D.: Suicide rates of men and women. *Omega,* 7: 95-101, 1976.

Durkheim, E.: *Suicide.* Glencoe: Free Press, 1951.

Farber, M. L.: *Theory of suicide.* New York: Funk & Wagnalls, 1968.

Geeken, M., and Gove, W. R.: *At home and at work: the family's allocation of labor.* Beverly Hills: Sage, 1983.

Gibbs, J. P., and Martin, W. T.: *Status integration and suicide.* Eugene: University of Oregon Press, 1964.

Heiman, M.: The police suicide. *Journal of Police Science & Administration,* 3: 267-273, 1975.

Henry, A. F., and Short, J. F.: *Suicide and homicide.* Glencoe: Free Press, 1954.

Kalish, R. A.: Suicide. *Bulletin of Suicidology,* December: 37-43, 1968.

Lester, D.: Completed suicide and females in the labor force. *Psychological Reports,* 32: 730, 1973.

Lester, D.: Suicide in police officers. *Police Chief,* 45(4): 17, 1978.

Li, F. B.: Suicide among chemists. *Archives of Environmental Health,* 19: 518-520, 1969.

Maris, R.: Suicide, status, and mobility in Chicago. *Social Forces,* 46: 246-256, 1967.

Merikangas, K.: Sex differences in depression. Paper presented at the Murray Center (Radcliffe College) Conference on Mental Health in Social Context. Cambridge, MA, May 1985.

Michelson, W.: *From sun to sun.* Totowa, NJ: Rowman & Allanheld, 1985, pp. 72-88.

Miley, J., and Micklin, M.: Structural change and the Durkheimian legacy. *American Journal of Sociology,* 78: 657-673, 1972.

Mortimer, J. T., and London, J.: The varying linkages of work and family. In P. Voydanoff (Ed.) *Work and Family.* Palo Alto: Mayfield, 1984.

Newman, J., Whittemore, K., and Newman, H.: Women in the labor force and suicide. *Social Problems,* 21: 220-230, 1973.

Pitts, F., Scholler, A., Rich, C., and Pitts, A.: Suicide among US women physicians, 1967-1972. *American Journal of Psychiatry,* 136: 694-696, 1979.

Platt, S.: Unemployment and suicide. *Social Science & Medicine,* 19: 93-115, 1984.

Robin, A. A., Brook, E. M., and Freeman-Browne, D. L.: Some aspects of suicide in psychiatric patients. *British Medical Journal,* 3: 424-425, 1968.

Robins, E., Gasner, S., Kayes, J., Wilkinson, R. H., and Murphy, G. E.: The communication of suicidal intent. *American Journal of Psychiatry,* 115: 724-733, 1959.

Rose, K., and Rosow, I.: Physicians who kill themselves. *Archives of General Psychiatry,* 29: 800-805, 1973.

Rushing, W.: Income, unemployment and suicide. *Sociological Quarterly,* 9: 493-503, 1968.

Simon, J. L.: The effect of income on the suicide rate. *American Journal of Sociology*, 74: 302-303, 1968.

Stack, S.: Suicide. *Social Forces*, 57: 644-653, 1978.

Staines, G. L., and Pleck, J. H.: *The impact of work schedules on the family*. Ann Arbor: University of Michigan Survey Research Center, Institute for Social Research, 1983.

Steffensmeier, R. H.: Suicide and the contemporary women: are male and female suicide rates converging? *Sex Roles*, 10: 613-631, 1984.

Stengel, E.: *Suicide and attempted suicide*. London, England: Penguin, 1964.

Steppacher, R., and Mausner, J.: Suicide in male and female physicians. *Journal of the American Medical Association*, 228: 323-328, 1974.

Tuckman, J., and Youngman, W. F.: A scale for assessing risk of attempted suicides. *Journal of Clinical Psychology*, 24: 17-19, 1968.

Verbrugge, L. M.: Women: social roles and health. In P. Berman and E. Ramey (Eds.), *Women: a developmental perspective*. Bethesda, MD: National Institutes of Health, 1982. (Publication No. 82-2298, pp. 49-78).

Waldron, I., and Herold, J.: Employment, attitudes toward employment and women's health. Paper presented at the meeting of the Society of Behavioral Medicine, Philadelphia, March 1984.

Whitlock, F. A., and Edwards, J. E.: Pregnancy and attempted suicide. *Comprehensive Psychiatry*, 9: 1-12, 1968.

Whitlock, F. A., and Schapira, K.: Attempted suicide in Newcastle-upon-Tyne. *British Journal of Psychiatry*, 113: 423-434, 1967.

Yeh, B. Y., and Lester, D.: The participation of females in the labor force and rates of personal violence (suicide and homicide). *Suicide & Life-Threatening Behavior*, in press: 1988.

Zung, W., and Moore, J.: Suicide potential in a normal adult population. *Psychosomatics*, 17: 37-41, 1976.

CHAPTER 5

THE THINKING PROCESSES
IN SUICIDAL WOMEN

CHARLES NEURINGER

THERE EXISTS a group of suicidologists who believe that the key to understanding and predicting suicide resides in the analysis of self-destructive individuals' patterns of organizing their thought processes. Such a cognition-oriented view arose out of disappointments in firmly tying down particular unequivocal relationships between motivational-personality variables and subsequent suicidal activity. (Because of these frustrations the field of Suicidology has moved in the direction of social engineering projects to prevent and inhibit suicide and away from explorations of the psychodynamics of self-destruction.) The analysis of cognitive patterns in suicidal individuals has proved to be useful in understanding the "inner" forces leading to self-selected death (Neuringer, 1976).

The "spiritual leader" of this group is Edwin S. Shneidman. In 1957, Shneidman suggested that there existed a pattern of cognitive organizations in certain individuals, that, if acted upon, would inevitably lead to suicidal choices. He called this pattern "Dichotomous Thinking." Dichotomous thinkers, he said, tend to organize their attitudinal systems in terms of dichotomies rather than continuities. Thus, an event, object, or relationship is conceptualized as either "good" or "bad," rather than somewhat in between these two alternatives. Reflections of this kind of thinking appeared in Charles Osgood's and Evelyn Walker's (1959) semantic analysis of real and simulated suicide notes. Osgood and Walker reported that the real note writers tended to use words like "always," "never," and "forever" to a much greater extent than did the fake note writers. In a classic case study in the annals of suicidology, Ludwig Binswanger (1958), when describing a young suicidal woman, reported that she had unrealistically high levels of aspiration and told of her constantly reiterated insistence that life was to her either perfect or terrible.

Neuringer (1964) found that suicidal males showed markedly high bipolar dichotomous organization of their interpersonal relations as compared to non-suicidal individuals. He found that for suicidal persons an initial positive attitude towards another person turned completely "sour" when a trivial dissonant piece of information was introduced into the relationship. The suicidal individuals could only conceptualize the relationship between themselves and others as only either extremely positive or extremely negative, and not anywhere in between.

Neuringer (1961, 1967, 1968, 1970, 1979a, 1979b) also expanded on the nature of suicidal thinking by demonstrating that extreme divergent bipolar attitudes towards life and death occurred as a corolary of dichotomous thinking (i.e., dichotomous thinking forces the individual to develop extreme and rigid bipolar feelings about these two states). The above cited research was conducted exclusively with suicidal males. For these individuals, the existence of dichotomous thinking and extreme polarization of life-death attitudes has been well established. The question arose as to whether such thinking patterns also exist in seriously suicidal women. Fatal suicidal activity in women is rare as compared to that of men. However, it also seems to be on the rise as more women enter the labor market (Davis, 1981; Frederick, 1985). In order to answer that question, Neuringer and Lettieri (1971, 1982) applied the dichotomous thinking and bipolar extremity evaluation procedures developed for males to women of varying levels of suicidality.

Attitudes towards life and death, and dichotomous thinking evaluations were gathered from suicidal women of variously rated lethality and from a crisis (but not suicidal) group. Four groups of women were used in their research. They were (1) a high suicidal lethality group, (2) a moderate suicidal lethality group, (3) a low suicidality group and (4) a zero lethality group. Lethality level was established by the use of the Los Angeles Suicide Prevention Center Lethality of Intent Rating Scale (Farberow, Heilig and Litman, 1968). The ratings were made by the Los Angeles Suicide Prevention Center staff.

All of the suicidal women were procured from that center. They were individuals who called in and then came to the facility. They were seen, evaluated, rated and asked to participate in the study. They were told that they would receive a certain amount of money ($2 for each day of participation) when they had completed all of their forms. They were asked to fill out a set of forms (which will be described later) every day for 21 days and mail it to the Suicide Prevention Center. Stamped and addressed envelopes were provided. The money was used as both a reward and a prod since they could not receive the funds until all of the data for 21 days were completed and had arrived in the mail. The continual gathering of data over a three week period was an innovation. It had not been done with male suicidal individuals. Neuringer and Lettieri felt that it was important to chart the course of cognitive states over time in order to evaluate their level of persistence.

The choice of 21 days for the crisis period was one that was dictated by several considerations. Pilot work had indicated that this time span was best for sustaining interest and cooperation. A calculated guess was also made as to how long after a suicidal crisis changes in attitude might be expected to appear. There is nothing in the literature indicating how long after a suicidial crisis the person remains basically self-destructive in orientation and outlook. There are, of course, individual differences in this matter, but clinical judgments indicated that three weeks was an ample time period. There does seem to be some data from the field of rehabilitation psychology (Shontz, 1965) on the duration of acute depressive reactions to severe physical crisis (e.g., loss of a limb) that indicated that three weeks was a crucial recovery period for these kinds of acute traumas. After that period the person either begins to reconstitute or becomes more morose and rejecting of his loss.

The suicidal women came to the Los Angeles Suicide Prevention Center with a variety of complaints. All of them were suicide threaterners (i.e., one could not uncover any overt suicidial behavior associated with their current crisis, although it many cases there had been histories of such activity). The nonsuicidal women were procured from a variety of sources. Some of them came into the Suicide Prevention Center with a crisis problem but were clearly not then, or previously, suicidal. Most nonsuicidal but crisis-affected women were procured at the University of California (Los Angeles) Neuropsychiatric Institute and various walk-in clinics in and around the Los Angeles area.

The women were asked to fill out a Semantic Differential and Daily Self-Lethality Report (to be described below). The Semantic Differential was composed of nine concepts, each with an identical set of 18 attendant bipolar scales (9 evaluative, 4 activity, and 5 potency scales). Seven of the concepts were not germane to the present study. Only the evaluative responses to two of the concepts (life and death) will be reported upon here. The participants were asked to rate these concepts along the 18 scales in terms of how they felt about them that day. This was done every day for 21 days. They were also asked to fill out a Daily Self-Lethality Report form for each of the 21 days. One of the items on that form was as follows: "During the last 24 hours I felt that the chances of my actually killing myself (committing suicide and ending my life) were: (1) Absent, (2) Very Low, (3) Low, (4) Low-Medium, (5) 50-50, (6) High-Medium, (7) High, (8) Very High, (9) Extra High (came very close to actually killing myself)."

The daily Self-Lethality Report forms were to be filled in and mailed to the Suicide Prevention Center along with the Semantic Differential forms every day for 21 consecutive days.

Neuringer and Lettieri were interested in the straightforward attitudes towards life and death, and the Semantic Differential data can be analyzed so as to yield scores ranging from +3 to (extremely positive) through 0 (neutral) to −3 (extremely negative). One could presume that the ideally well-adjusted happy person would rate life as +3 and death as a −3.

The Semantic Differential data can also be analyzed in terms of the amount of dichotomous thinking existing in the individual. This was done by assigning a score of 3 for extreme judgments, such as "very good" or "very bad," a score of 2 for moderate judgments such as "moderately beautiful" or "moderately ugly," a score of 1 for mild judgments, and a score of 0 for neutral judgments. The more extreme the judgment, the higher the dichotomous thinking score. The item described above on the Daily Self-Lethality Report form was correlated with the daily attitude and dichotomous thinking data presented by each woman in order to ascertain whether there was an interrelationship between the variables (i.e., to evaluate the influence of how suicidal one feels on attitudes towards life and death and the extent of dichotomous thinking). In this way information was procured about the day-to-day fluctuations in suicidality and the cognitive organization among the suicidal groups.

The data gathered from that study were very illuminating. [For a detailed report of that investigation, the reader is referred to Neuringer and Lettieri (1971, 1982)]. The High lethality group consistently rated life negatively throughout the 21 days and were more consistent than the other women. The moderate lethality group felt that life was mostly negative early in the period, but by the 14th day, it had changed to positive feelings about life. The low lethality group, like the moderate lethality group, was initially despairing of life, but after the 8th day it tended to see life in a positive manner during the rest of the 21 day period. The zero lethality group was consistently positive in its attitudes towards life. Although one can conclude that the moderate, low, and zero lethality women can be described as being generally positive about life, none of them were very ebullient about it.

Statistical analysis of this data indicated that the high lethality women were clearly different from the other groups. They had a significantly more negative attitude towards life than the other three groups and also the attitude persisted and was maintained across time. This characteristic was evidenced only in the high lethality group. None of the other women showed this trend. The attitudes towards death among the groups was startling and disturbing. The high lethality women praised death most of all, and for them it had positive value. Death was consistently rated negative by all the other groups. Just as it was observed for the life attitude data, the high lethality group stood out in comparison with the other women. Once more there did not seem to be any meaningful shifts over time from the initial rating of death by any of the groups.

An analysis was made of the day-to-day simultaneous attitudes towards life and death for each day. This was done in order to evaluate the disparity between the two attitudes. Other work in the area of suicidal cognition (Neuringer, 1968) had suggested that the gap between attitudes towards life and death may be an important clue to the emergence of suicidal behavior. The greatest amount of divergency between life and death was found for the high lethality women. It is of crucial interest that the life-death order was reversed among the high lethality women from that of the other women. For all the groups of less than high lethality, life was rated positively, and death was rated negatively. The high lethality group was the only one that conceived of death as positive and life as negative.

There also seems to be a definite divergency continuum. The least suicidal women seemed to make a clearly defined distinction in their minds about their attitudes towards life and death (i.e., life is good, and death is bad). As women move up the suicidality lethality scale, the divergency becomes less distinct, but the value hierarchy of life and death remains the same. Finally, when the high lethality levels were reached, there is a crossover, and a radical shift towards the opposite poles occurred. Death became positive and life became negative, and there is a clear divergency between the reversed polarity of life and death attitudes.

The high lethality women consistently showed the greatest amount of dichotomous thinking of all the groups. The zero lethality women seem to have evidenced the least amount of dichotomous thinking throughout the same period. No differences over time were noted. It appears that all the women were consistent in their dichotomous thinking levels throughout the 21 day period. It can be reasonably concluded that the high lethality women were different from the other groups in how they organized their thinking about the nature of the world. For them, objects, people, concepts, ideas, etc. are seen in terms of extremes with little or no moderation of their attitudes. A more balanced view was held by the other groups with the highest level of moderation appearing for the zero lethality women. The dichotomous thinking scores of the high lethality group were consistently higher across the 21 days than those of the other groups. The zero lethality women showed the least amount of dichotomous thinking of all the participants. Once more there does not seem to be much of a change in the amount of dichotomous thinking over time. This fact leads one to suspect that a fundamental cognitive style that is not affected by type of concept or temporal flow exists for all of the women. All of the them seemed to have established an initial level of dichotomous thinking and maintained it during the evaluation period.

It appeared that life and death attitudes seem to be more sensitive to (i.e., affected by) feelings of suicidality than does dichotomous thinking. Reported daily levels of suicidality influenced and affected attitudes towards life and death (and vice versa). The extent of the relationship increases in proportion to the level of lethality (i.e., the low and moderate women had the lowest and the high lethality group had the highest correlations between self-rated lethality and both the life and death concepts). This seems to imply that all suicidal groups' feelings of self-destructiveness (i.e., wanting to die) are functionally related to attitudes towards life and death to a significant extent, but it relates to the high lethality group most of all (i.e., when they are feeling particularly self-destructive, death is perceived as even more positive and life as even more negative than when they are feeling less suicidal).

The high lethality group personnel were the only women who had a significant correlation between self-rated lethality and their levels of dichotomous thinking. Their uniqueness in this matter adds support to the contention that they are a group distinctly different from all other suicidal participants. When they are feeling more depressed than usual, unhappy and wanting to die, they (alone among all the suicidal groups) are the only ones to think more dichotomously than when they are feeling less suicidal.

A series of inferences can be drawn from the results of the Neuringer and Lettieri study. It seems reasonable to conclude that the assessments towards life and death can be a useful device for identifying, predicting and preventing suicide. There seems to be a difference in (a) how suicidal women of differing lethality levels conceive of their lives and deaths, and (b) that these self-destructive persons' conceptions are not completely linear. The relationship between lethality level and attitude is linear only up to a point. Normal individuals up to moderately suicidal persons see life as being more positive than death and death as more negative than life. The amount of "moreness" is inversly related to the suicidal lethality (i.e., the less suicidal the individual, the more life is positive and the more death is negative, and vice versa). The divergency between life and death is also inversly related to lethality level. The less suicidal woman sees a greater difference between life and death than the moderately suicidal woman. However, from the normal to the moderately suicidal person, the difference is in the amount of divergency, but not in the order of the two concepts.

However, beyond the level of moderate lethality, there is a radical reversal. The world of the highly suicidal woman becomes topsy-turvy. Life and death change places and take completely different positions in the value hierarchy. Death becomes good and life is bad, and they are perceived as being distinct from each other (i.e., they are seen as clear and definite alternatives). When that happens, a threshold has been crossed. At that moment, the person becomes validly suicidal (i.e., truly interested in her own demise), rather than being primarily motivated to manipulate others or cry for help. One is dealing with a completely new order of motives and cognitive organization when confronted by the high suicidial risk as opposed to being faced with persons of lower suicidal lethality. The highly suicidal woman is in a different world than the other women. This conclusion implies that treatment programs for the serious suicidal risks person have to be different from those instituted for lesser suicidally lethal people. It may be that answering a presumed cry for help is not the way to save their lives. Restraint and a whole social engineering program may be what is needed.

The dichotomous thinking findings lead to conclusions similar to those drawn from the attitude data. The high suicidal lethality women stand out as unique from the other self-destructive women. High suicidal risk persons think far more dichotomously than the other people in this study (i.e., they think differently than the other persons in that most everything is conceived of in terms of extremes to a greater extent than most people). It is as if for them, objects, thoughts, ideas, values, things, people, and so on, if they are not completely beautiful and ecstatic, then they can only be completely ugly and disgusting. Since the world can never meet such grandiose expectations, people have consciously or unconsciously learned not to expect very much and take and enjoy things as they are. High suicidial risk persons do not seem to have learned this primary lesson of life and expect perfection. They concomitantly also have inordinately high levels of aspiration. And when they are disappointed (as surely they must be), they respond as if they had been utterly rejected. They become depressed and unhappy as an inevitable consequence of their high levels of dichotomous thinking. Extreme bipolar dichotomous thinking is dangerous because it jeopardizes one's capacity to live acceptably in the real world. The overwhelming and characteristic presence of this factor in highly suicidial persons may well serve as a criticial element in the definition of suicide.

There was neither a significant accretion or diminution of attitudes towards life and death or dichotomous thinking over time. This suggests that dichotomous cognitions are an ingrained and resistant-to-change way of seeing the world and of relating the self to the environment. What is being suggested is that dichotomous thinking is an essential characteristic of people (i.e., it is a dispositional quality, very much like "intelligence").

This leads one to raise the specter of a "suicidal personality" with all the implications of a motivational and cognitive system that is organized towards a very high probability of successful, self-destructive behavior. Unless one can find evidence that dichotomous thinking is not related to high suicidial risk or that it is amenable to change, one may have to accept the possibility that there are people who are suicidal because their cognitive organizations make them that way (i.e., they are not just reacting to situational stress alone, but to an internal coding system that categorizes stress as insoluble, and therefore completely and forever unending—a condition that leads to exit from the world). For these people "restraint" and a dependency-generating social engineering may be the way to save their lives. Litman (1963) has already remarked that therapy with the high suicidal risk must consist primarily of being very directive in dealing with the patient.

The role of affect needs to be commented upon here in relationship to the difference between the high suicidal risk woman and the lesser suicidal women. All of the attitudes towards life and death of the groups in this study changed with variations in their day-to-day affect levels. But the greatest amount of change occurred for the high suicidal lethality women as compared to the other people in this study. They were also the only group whose dichotomous thinking was significantly related to their affect state (i.e., their way of conceptualizing and organizing their experiences became either more or less dichotomous depending upon how they felt at any given moment). That fact may be yet another indication of the uniqueness of the high suicidal risks person. Dichotomous thinking may be a kind of suicidal thermometer.

The finding of the lack of change during the 21 day period in bipolarization of life-death attitudes and dichotomous thinking in the seriously suicidal women is somewhat disturbing. It augers poorly for the futures of these women. Dichotomous thinking imposes inflexibility and polarized thinking on suicidal individuals. It may be that the inflexibility and polarization associated with dichotomous thinking are what perpetuates and maintains for long periods of time a high level of crisis. If the above is true, highly suicidal women are caught in a web that appears to be seamless and never-ending (i.e., the pain never diminishes long enough for the person to feel better). If the cognitive style does indeed constantly keep the "emotional pot" boiling, it may explain why suicidal individuals feel so hopeless and why they have such difficulties envisioning a future in which they will feel better (Neuringer and Levenson, 1972).

REFERENCES

Binswanger, L.: The case of Ellen West. In R. May, E. Angel and H. F. Ellenberger (Eds.). *Existence*. New York: Basic Books, 1958.

Davis, R. A.: Female labor force participation, status intergration and suicide, 1950-1969. *Suicide and Life Threatening Behavior*, 11: 111-113, 1981.

Farberow, N. L., Heilig, S. M. & Litman, R. E.: *Techniques in crisis intervention: A training manual.* Los Angeles: Delmar, 1968.

Frederick, C.J.: An introduction and overview of youth suicide. In M. L. Peck, N. L. Farberow and R. E. Litman (Eds.). *Youth suicide.* New York: Springer, 1985.

Litman, R. E.: Emergency response to potential suicide. *Journal of the Michigan State Medical Society*, 62: 68-72, 1963.

Neuringer, C.: Dichotomous evaluations in suicidal individuals. *Journal of Consulting Psychology*, 25: 445-449, 1961.

Neuringer, C.: Reactions to interpersonal crisis in suicidal individuals. *Journal of General Psychology*, 71: 47-55, 1964.

Neuringer, C.: The cognitive organization of meaning in suicidal individuals. *Journal of General Psychology*, 76: 91-100, 1967.

Neuringer, C.: Divergencies between attitudes towards life and death among suicidal, psychosomatic and normal hospitalized patients. *Journal of Consulting and Clinical Psychology,* 32: 59-63, 1968.

Neuringer, C.: Changes in attitudes towards life and death during recovery from a serious suicide attempt. *Omega,* 1: 301-309, 1970.

Neuringer, C.: Current developments in the study of suicidal thinking. In E. S. Shneidman (Ed.). *Suicidology: Current developments.* New York: Grune and Stratton, 1976.

Neuringer, C.: The semantic perception of life, death and suicide. *Journal of Clinical Psychology,* 35: 255-258, 1979a.

Neuringer, C.: The relationship between life and death among individuals of varying levels of suicidality. *Journal of Consulting and Clinical Psychology,* 47: 407-408, 1979b.

Neuringer, C., & Lettieri, D. J.: Cognition, attitude and affect in suicidal individuals. *Life Threatening Behavior,* 1: 106-124, 1971.

Neuringer, C., & Lettieri, D. J.: *Suicidal women: Their thinking and feeling patterns.* New York: Gardner Press, 1982.

Neuringer, C., & Levenson, M.: Time perception in suicidal individuals. *Omega,* 3: 181-186, 1972.

Shneidman, E. S.: The logic of suicide. In E. S. Shneidman and N. L. Farberow (Eds.). *Clues to suicide.* New York: McGraw-Hill, 1957.

Shontz, F. C.: Reactions to crisis. *Volta Review,* 67: 364-370, 1965.

CHAPTER 6

THE SUICIDE NOTES OF WOMEN

ANTOON A. LEENAARS

UNDERSTANDING suicidal phenomena—like understanding all complicated human acts—is a complex endeavour, involving information and insights drawn from many sources. Shneidman and Farberow (1957), Maris (1981) and others have suggested the following alternatives: statistics, third party interviews, the study of nonfatal suicide attempters and documents (including *personal documents*). All of these have their limitations (Leenaars, 1988a, Maris, 1981); yet, each source of data has brought social scientists closer to understanding the event. Although there is considerable controversy around the admissibility of introspective accounts as opposed to objective reports (Runyan, 1982; Windelband, 1904), Allport (1942) noted that personal documents have a significant place in social science research. Allport cited some shortcomings in the use of personal documents; e.g., unrepresentativeness of sample, self-deception, blindness to motives, errors of memory; however, he made a clear case for their use citing the following: learning about the person, advancing both nomothetic and ideographic research, and aiding in the aims of science in general—understanding, prediction, and control. As an interesting historical footnote to Allport's work in the 1940's, he wrote about diaries, memories, logs, letters, autobiographies, but it did not occur to him to think of perhaps the most personal document of all: suicide notes.

Suicide notes are the ultra personal documents (Leenaars, 1988a; Shneidman, 1980). They are the unsolicited productions of the suicidal person, usually written minutes before the suicidal death. They are an invaluable starting point for comprehending the suicidal act and for understanding the special features about people who actually commit suicide and what they share in common with the rest of us who have only been drawn to imagine it (Leenaars, 1988a; Leenaars and Balance, 1984a; Shneidman, 1980, 1985; Shneidman and Farberow, 1957).

Early research (e.g., Wolff, 1931) on suicide notes largely utilized an anecdotal approach that incorporated descriptive information. Subsequent methods of study have primarily included classification analysis and content analysis. Currently, there are over 60 published articles on suicide notes; an extensive review with an annotated bibliography has been presented elsewhere (Leenaars, 1988a). Only a very few of these studies have utilized a theoretical-conceptual analysis despite the belief, since the first formal study of suicide notes, that such contributions offer a rich potential (Shneidman and Farberow, 1957). In a series of studies spanning the last 10 years (e.g., Leenaars, 1979, 1985, 1986, 1987a & b, 1988a; Leenaars & Balance, 1981, 1984a, b & c; Leenaars, Balance, Wenckstern & Rudzinski, 1985), the author and his colleagues introduced a logical, empirical approach to suicide notes which not only presented a method for the theoretical analysis of suicide notes but was also calculated to augment the effectiveness of previous controls.

Essentially, this method which has been outlined in detail elsewhere (Leenaars, 1988a; Leenaars & Balance, 1984a) calls for the notes to be treated as an archival source and subjected to the scrutiny of *control* hypothesis, following an *ex post facto* research design (Kerlinger, 1964). Suicide notes are recast in *different* theoretical contexts (hypotheses, theories, models, etc.) for which lines of evidence of each of these positions can then be pursued in the data, utilizing Carnap's logical and empirical procedures (1931/1959) for such investigations. These positivistic procedures call for the translating of theoretical formulations into observable (specific) *protocol sentences* in order to test the formulations. The protocol sentences are the meaning of the theory as they are matched empirically, by independent judges, with the actual data. Next, conclusions are developed from the verified protocol sentences. The method allows predictive validity or its equivalent to be introduced into the investigation of suicide notes and also allows testing between theoretical positions, discriminations within theoretical positions and facilitation of model building.

To date, the theories of 10 suicidologists have been investigated (Leenaars, 1988a). Specifically, studies of A. Adler, L. Binswanger, S. Freud, C. G. Jung, K. A. Menninger, G. Kelly, H. A. Murray, E. S. Shneidman, H. S. Sullivan and G. Zilboorg have been undertaken.

From these investigations, 23 protocol sentences were found that highly predicted (described) the content of suicide notes (i.e., one standard deviation above the mean of all observations which was equivalent to being observed in ⅔ of the notes) and 18 protocol sentences that significantly discriminated genuine suicide notes from simulated suicide notes (i.e., control data). Both sources of information have utility in understanding suicide. These same sentences were subsequently reduced to a meaningful empirical nosology (Leenaars, 1988b). Since five sentences both predicted and discriminated the content, the 36 individual sentences were grouped into eight discrete clusters, utilizing a Cluster Analysis (SAS Institute, 1985). The eight clusters identified by a word or short phrase are as follows: I. Unbearable Psychological Pain; II. Interpersonal Relations; III. Rejection-Aggression; IV. Inability to Adjust; V. Indirect Expressions; VI. Identification-Egression; VII. Ego; and VIII. Cognitive Constriction. One protocol sentence was unassigned. The Appendix presents the significant clusters (including the name of the suicidologist from whom the original protocol sentence was derived and whether the sentence is a predictive and/or discriminative clue).

The first controlled study of suicide notes indicated that the dynamics or reaction patterns may vary with critical demographic variables (Shneidman & Farberow, 1957). However, although some studies have investigated age (reviewed by Leenaars, 1988a), only a few studies have subsequently examined sex, despite the continued research that sex differences may exist in suicide as evident in this volume and noted elsewhere (e.g., Leenaars, 1987b; Lester, 1979, 1984). One major reason for this neglect is the lack of availability of data. The major source for previous research in this area (Shneidman & Farberow, 1957) supplied an archive of notes written only by males. Recently, a new published archive (Leenaars, 1988a) has been made available to allow researchers to develop their own study of suicide notes written by both sexes. It is our hope that researchers will subsequently investigate both male and female notes in their investigations.

Although not the primary focus of the research, Cohen and Fiedler (1974) and Lester and Reeve (1982) reported the following sex differences in suicide notes: females appear to be less direct and less negative in their communications about the forthcoming suicide; females exhibit greater concern for others whom they know interpersonally; females express greater negative emotions, specifically despondency, grief, and disappointment; and females appear to be more disorganized in their writings. However, Leenaars (1987a & b, 1988) has recently questioned some of these findings. Utilizing a protocol analysis with a sample of notes written by females and males drawn from across the adult life span, no differences were found on the above variables, reported by Cohen and Fiedler (1974) and Lester and Reeve (1982). Although this research is too extensive to be cited here in detail, briefly this research indicated no psychological differences in males and females for perturbation, relations, cognitions regarding an afterlife, cognitions regarding self, truncated cognitions, the experience of trauma, fear of insanity, idea of cessation or egression, early life stresses, the communication of lethality, long term instability, and conscious intention related to a recent stress. Other researchers, reviewed elsewhere (Leenaars, 1988a), have also reported no differences in the suicide notes of males and females. The primary purpose of this study is to identify *psychological* differences between females and males for suicide based upon a protocol analysis of their notes. The suicide notes of both sexes will be investigated from the individual protocol sentences and their clusters, presented in the Appendix. The study, thus, can be seen as constituting one of the most extensive studies of the suicide notes of males and females in the current literature.

Method

Two independent individuals, who have graduate degrees in psychology and are currently in clinical practice, served as judges. These judges had no previous experience with the protocol method. No demographic or other information about the suicide notes were provided. They were asked to verify whether the protocol sentences (presented in the Appendix) did, in fact, occur in 40 suicide notes, 20 notes representing each sex. These 40 notes constitute a sub-group of 60 suicide notes that were selected from a sample of over 400 suicide notes. Since previous research (e.g., Leenaars, 1987b) indicated that age is a significant variable, the notes were selected on the basis of age and sex. The specified age ranges were as follows: Young Adulthood (18-25 yrs.), Middle Adulthood (25-55 yrs.) and Late Adulthood (55 yrs. and up). The male-female sample of notes includes all the notes that were capable of being matched within a 3 year-age-range, resulting in seven pairs of matched notes for Young Adults, six pairs for Middle Adults and seven pairs for Late Adults. Thus, the female-male sample represents the three major recognized age groups in adulthood (Erikson, 1963, 1968; Colarusso & Nemiroff, 1981; Kimmel, 1974) almost in equal fashion, virtually eliminating age as a confounding variable.

The overall mean age of the sample is 41.59; the age range is 18-77; and the notes were written between 1966 and 1983.

Both the notes and protocol sentences were presented in a randomized order, and the judges were instructed:

> Enclosed you will find a collection of suicide notes. Your task will be to verify whether the statements provided below correspond or compare to the contents of the suicide notes. The statements provided below are a classification of the possible content of suicide notes. You are to determine whether the contents in the suicide notes are a particular or specific instance of that classification or not. Your comparison should be *observable;* however, the classifications may be more abstract than the specific instances. Thus you will have to make judgements about whether particular contents of a note are included in a given classification or not. Your task is to either conclude yes or no.

Results

A coefficient of concordance for the complete set of notes (Siegel, 1956) of .76 ($\times 2$ (35, n = 60) = 53.2, p < .05) indicated substantial inter-judge reliability.

Chi-square tests for two independent samples (Siegel, 1956) for each protocol sentence and an Analysis of Variance on the relevant discrete clusters [Cluster Analysis, Varclus procedure (SAS Institute, Inc., 1985)] produced *no* significant results. Table 1 presents the proportion of each cluster found in the notes.

Table 1

PROPORTION OF EACH
OF THE EIGHT PSYCHOLOGICAL CLASSIFICATIONS
FOUND IN THE SUICIDE NOTES FOR EACH SEX

Cluster	Female	Male
I Unbearable Psychological Pain	85.25%	79.65%
II Interpersonal Relations	40.16%	24.11%
III Rejection-Aggression	24.30%	19.25%
IV Inability to Adjust	39.40%	47.52%
V Indirect Expressions	55.66%	57.41%
VI Identification-Egression	24.10%	30.63%
VII Ego	34.57%	30.64%
VIII Cognitive Constriction	59.40%	66.52%

Discussion

Suicide is best understood as a multidimensional human malaise (Shneidman, 1985). It would seem most accurate to define suicide as an event with biological (including biochemical, neuropsychological), socio-cultural, interpersonal, philosophical/existential, and psychological aspects. From a psychological point of view, suicide has been structured differently by various suicidologists. Recently, Leenaars (1988a) attempted to define suicide in terms of suicide notes by studying ten suicidologists. From this work, a number of predictive (23) and differentiating (18) variables were isolated that could be used to understand suicide within a psychological framework. These same sentences were subsequently reduced to eight discrete clusters (Leenaars, 1988b). Specifically, suicide can be defined psychologically from the following variables: Unbearable Pain; Interpersonal Relations; Rejection-Aggression; Inability to Adjust; Indirect Expression; Identification-Egression; Ego; and Cognitive Constriction. The current study suggests that there are *no* sex differences on these variables in suicide notes and, by implication, suicide.

Are women's suicides really different from men's? The current study and previous ones on psychological characteristics in suicide notes (Leenaars, 1987a & b, 1988a) suggest no. Thus, one can cautiously generalize across both males and females critical *psychological* characteristics in suicide notes and, by implication, suicide. There appear to be no sex differences on such issues as "I love you," "I am in unbearable pain," "I am hopeless and helpless," "I cannot cope," and, "This is the only way out for me."

These negative results, however, do raise again a question about the findings of Cohen and Fiedler (1974) and Lester and Reeve (1982) that females express greater negative emotions; females show greater interpersonal concern; females appear to be more disorganized. In our sample, both males and females exhibited heightened emotions, interpersonal concerns, constriction and other fallacious logic. It may well be that males are as emotional, interpersonally troubled and constricted in their thoughts as women in their suicide notes and, by implication, suicide (although the mode(s) of expression may differ due to gender role).

Possible reasons for the discrepancies in the literature include methodological differences (e.g., methods) and sampling differences. Although previously, differences in method of analysis of the notes were construed as the most likely reason (Leenaars, 1987a), it may well be that sampling problems are equally (or even more) important. The basis for this conclusion is that although there appear to be no known sex differences in the suicide notes of males and females if age is controlled for in the sample, a sex by age interaction exists (Leenaars, 1987a, 1988b). To date the following have been noted: Young and Middle Adult females appear to exhibit greater confusion regarding their self cognitions than their male counterparts; Young and Middle Adult females appear to exhibit a greater concern about their relations than their male counterparts although the reverse is evident in Late Adulthood; i.e., Late Adult males appear to be more concerned about their relationships than Late Adult females; Young Adult females appear to be more preoccupied in their notes about their lack of constructive tendencies than their male counterparts (although both sexes in this age group exhibit this characteristic more frequently than other adults); and Young Adult males (compared to their female counterparts) appear to be more frequently judged from their notes to be unable to adjust; e.g., their notes are more consistent with a defined social disorder (although again both sexes in Young Adulthood exhibit this characteristic more frequently than individuals in Middle and Late Adulthood). These results suggest a number of important conclusions including that some of the previous reported findings regarding overall sex differences in suicide notes (Cohen & Fiedler, 1974; Lester & Reeve, 1982) may have been a function of the age ranges and sex in the samples and not sex alone. For example, the concern about relations is clearly more evident for females in some age ranges but not all. Future research on sex in suicide notes and, by implication, suicide must consider sex by age interactions in the studies and not simple overall sex differences. Indeed, research consistently supports the need to adopt a life-span perspective in understanding suicide for both males and females.

Our results also raise an important question in light of the generally accepted male-female ratio of 3 to 1 in completed suicide which has been substantiated in recent research (McIntosh & Jewell, 1986). Why should males kill themselves three times more often than females? As previously noted, suicide is a multifaceted event. Explanations for the sex difference in completed suicide have included variation in method (Lester, 1984; Leenaars & Lester, 1988), biological differences (Baino, 1967; Lester, 1979), psychiatric nosological differences (Lester, 1970), and sociological differences (Davis, 1981; Lester, 1984; Linehan, 1973; Ornstein, 1983); yet, each suicide is also a psychological event. Further research on psychological factors is warranted, although it may be wise for psychologists and other mental health professionals to take special note of the fact that suicide like other complicated human acts may be influenced by a number of aspects especially gender role (e.g., Chesler, 1972; Gilligan, 1982; Goldberg, 1976; Greenglass, 1982). As Greenglass (1982) noted:

> Since the beginning of recorded history, being male or female has been one of the most significant defining characteristics of a person. Sex and gender not only determine the kinds of experiences people have, but they also significantly influence the way people perceive and act toward each other. Moreover socio-cultural expectations have been integrated into elaborate gender-role systems which have an enormous impact on all areas of psychological and social functioning (p. 256).

In that regard, it appears that completed suicide is more a hazard of being male than female in *our* society [since other patterns appear to exist in other cultures (Counts, 1987)]. Method differences, psychiatric nosological differences and possibly even some biological differences can be construed to be related to gender role/sociological differences. Since we have found no overall sex differences, an important question can be asked: Are the high rates of completed suicide in males more influenced by gender roles (and/or other aspects) than psychological factors?

Echoing the views of Tomlinson-Keasey, Warren, and Elliot (1986), it is important to note that variables identified in the present study are certainly not the only psychological variables that might prompt someone to commit suicide. Other variables, not used in the present study, could certainly generate other findings. The variables examined here are ones that had been derived from only ten suicidologists; yet, *these* 10 individuals are generally recognized as having given us a rich history of theory about suicide.

An inherent problem in suicidology is obtaining adequate data (Maris, 1981); the study of suicide notes itself has a number of specific limitations. Only about 12 to 15 percent of suicides — males and females — leave notes (Leenaars, 1988a; Shneidman, 1985; Shneidman and Farberow, 1957). Thus, the conclusions about the psychology of suicide from suicide notes may contain some biases. However, since the first systematic study of suicide notes, no differences have been reported between individuals who leave notes and those who have not. Stengel (1964) suggested that writers of suicide notes may differ from the majority only in being good communicators. Other questions about the usefulness of suicide notes are as follows: whether an acutely suicidal individual provides a clear vs. a distorted communication; whether an individual can give only a partial vs. a complete account of the suicide; and whether the notes in a sample are representative of all suicide notes. Despite such problems, the research on suicide notes has been historically useful in describing the suicide as that individual is at the final throes of the life vs. death decision (Leenaars, 1988a; Lester, 1983; Maris, 1981; Shneidman, 1985).

To summarize, a sample of suicide notes written by females are presented verbatim, except identification changes. They let us know what it was like for these women at the last minute of their lives — .

Young Adulthood:

1.) Hello Sweetie

> I just wanted to tell you I still love you very much. Sweetie I'll always love you very much.
>
> My God, I don't know how all this happen but it did. I wish it never did happen. All I know it hurts real bad just thinking of it makes me cry and say why. I never though you would do this to me.
>
> Byi my Lady I love you forever,
>
> P.S. talk

Byi

> You're always be
> part of me and thought
> Sue I just want you to know I love you very much You know I still love you sweetie, I don't understand how all this happened, but you know what, I wish this would never have happened. Sue it hurts me very much. Just thinking of what happened makes me wonder why. I never thought you would do this to me! Sweetie I miss you.

Respectfully
Mary

P.S. I love you Sweetie

2.) Dearest Bill,

> "No matter what you think I've love you so completely me life is over now that you're going. Just the thought of you coming home from work, you gave me a thrill walking in the house. And not to have you with me anymore is more than I can bear. Forgive me, if you can. It has all been my fault for not being a wife first, a mother second. Because I would end up, embarrassing you, as you say, because I want you with me forever and I know that's no more for me. I love you so much."

Mary

Honey,

"_____ is a very good and lovable child. Give her a chance to love you as she has me. Take good care of her, please."

Mary

_____,

"Call _____ over to get me up."

Mom

Dear _____ & _____ & _____,

I'm sorry for all the trouble I've caused. I would love to be here for the baby, but I would be no good for any one any more. I love all my children so much. _____, _____, _____ his birth certificate and all the other certificates are on the shelf in the closet in my room in the insurance envelope. I wish I had something to leave you besides grief. Forgive me. I love you."

Mother

Middle Adulthood

3.) Bill,

I took 33 sleeping pills—I just cant go on feeling as I have the last three weeks. Love Mary, all I have is yours

Mary

4.) To whom it may concern:

I do not want any life sustaining equipment used on me. I do not want interveinous feeding or enemas. Use nothing at all to keep me alive. No one is to over-ride this request. It doesn't need to be signed or stamped by a Notary Republic.

There is to be no funeral.

Signed by me: Mary Smith

P.S. Do not let any of this get into the newspapers or any news.

To My Loved Ones:

I just couldn't take the pain any longer. The Doctors couldn't help me. Tell everyone it was a heart attack.

I am so sorry. I love you all so much. (over) Thanks for your deep concern and trying to help. I had no idea you cared so much. Please don't hate me for this. I love you. I love you all.

Mary

CARD: Don't let them take me to the morgue. I took sleeping pills. Have Dr. Smith sign the death certificate.

CARD: To Whom It May Concern:

If I should go into a coma, use no life sustaining equipment on me. I do not want intervenous feeding or enemas. Use nothing at all to keep me alive. No one is to over-ride this request. No funeral. It is my wish.

Mary Smith

CARD: Don't call the police. Call this mortuary:/Name and Tel. No./. No funeral.

CARD:

Dearest Bill:

I am so sorry. I wanted to hang in there for your sake but I couldn't take it any longer.

I love you so much.

Mary

CARD: Flush all my pills down the toilet so no kids will get hold of them in the trash. Throw away all the creams in the bathroom.

CARD: Bury me in this dress.

Late Adulthood:

5.) Dear Bill:

I know you are going to feel responsible for what I am about to do — This was inevitable and our being together for seven months only delayed it — when you get yourself straightened out, you should be able to find some peace of mind — I have so, I wish we could have found it together.

The little card attached to this note lists some medicine that _____ will has to have. Will you please get it for him, and, Bill, try to see he has a good home, he's been such good company for me. Also, will you kind of "stnad by" mother for me? She's going to take this hard — I'm sorry to hurt her — I'm sorry to hurt anyone — but it is what I have to do. I'm so tired.

Goodbye, Bill.

Mary

P.S. The laundry slip is for your shirts — they'll be ready Wednesday.

6.) 12:00 P.M.

I can't begin to explain what goes on in my mind it as though there's a tension pulling in all directions. I've gotten so I despise myself for the existence I've made for myself I've every reason for, but I can't see, to content myself with anything. If I don't do this or some other damned thing, I feel as tho' I'm going to have a nervous collapse.

May God forgive me, and you too, for what I am doing to you, my parents who have always tried so beautifully to understand me. It was futile, for I never quite understood myself. I love you all very much.

Mary

REFERENCES

Allport, G.: *The use of personal documents in psychological science.* New York: Social Science Research Council, 1942.

Baino, A.: Criminal abortion deaths, illegitimate pregnancy deaths and suicides in pregnancy. *American Journal of Obstetrics and Gynecology,* 98: 356-367, 1967.

Carnap, R.: Psychology in physical language. In A. Ayer (Ed.), *Logical positivism.* New York: Free Press, 1959. (Original published in 1931).

Chesler, P.: *Women & madness*. New York: Avon Books, 1972.

Cohen, S., & Fiedler, J.: Content analyses of multiple messages in suicide notes. *Suicide and Life-Threatening Behavior*, 4: 75-95, 1974.

Colarusso, C., & Nemiroff, R.: *Adult development*. New York: Plenum, 1981.

Counts, D.: Female suicide and wife abuse: A cross-cultural perspective. *Suicide and Life-Threatening Behavior*, 17: 194-204, 1987.

Davis, R.: Female labor force participation, status integration and suicide; 1950-1969. *Suicide and Life-Threatening Behavior*, 11: 111-123, 1981.

Erikson, E.: *Childhood and society*, (2nd ed.). New York: Norton, 1963.

Erikson, E.: *Identity: Youth and crisis*. New York: Norton, 1968.

Gilligan, C.: *In a different voice*. Cambridge: Harvard University Press, 1982.

Goldberg, H.: *The hazards of being male*. New York: Signet, 1976.

Greenglass, E.: *A world of difference*. New York: Wiley, 1982.

Kerlinger, F.: *Foundations of behavioral research*. New York: Holt, Rinehart & Winston, 1964.

Kimmel, D.: *Adulthood and aging*. New York: Wiley, 1974.

Leenaars, A.: *A Study of the manifest content of suicide notes from three different theoretical perspectives: L. Binswanger, S. Freud, and G. Kelly*. Unpublished Ph.D. Dissertation. University of Windsor, Canada, 1979.

Leenaars, A.: Freud's and Shneidman's formulations of suicide investigated through suicide notes. In E. Shneidman (Chair), *Suicide notes and other personal documents in psychological science*. Symposium conducted at the meeting of the American Psychological Association, Los Angeles, 1985.

Leenaars, A.: A brief note on the latent content in suicide notes. *Psychological Reports*, 59: 640-642, 1986.

Leenaars, A.: An empirical investigation of Shneidman's formulations regarding suicide: age & sex. *Suicide and Life-Threatening Behavior*, 17: 233-250, 1987a.

Leenaars, A.: Are women's suicides really different from men's? *Women & Health*, in press, 1987b.

Leenaars, A.: *Suicide notes*. New York: Human Sciences Press, 1988a.

Leenaars, A.: Suicide across the adult life-span: An archival study. Submitted for publication, 1988b.

Leenaars, A., & Balance, W.: A predictive approach to the study of manifest content in suicide notes. *Journal of Clinical Psychology*, 37: 50-52, 1981.

Leenaars, A., & Balance, W.: A logical empirical approach to the study of the manifest content in suicide notes. *Canadian Journal of Behavioral Science*, 16: 248-256, 1984a.

Leenaars, A., & Balance, W.: A predictive approach to Freud's formulations regarding suicide. *Suicide and Life-Threatening Behavior*, 14: 275-283, 1984b.

Leenaars, A., & Balance, W.: A predictive approach to suicide notes of young and old people from Freud's formulations regarding suicide. *Journal of Clinical Psychology*, 40: 1362-1364, 1984c.

Leenaars, A., Balance, W., Wenckstern, S., & Rudzinski, D.: An empirical investigation of Shneidman's formulations regarding suicide. *Suicide and Life-Threatening Behavior*, 15: 184-195, 1985.

Leenaars, A., & Lester, D.: The significance of the method chosen for suicide in understanding the psychodynamics of the suicidal individual. Submitted for publication, 1988.

Lester, D.: Suicide, sex and mental disorder. *Psychological Reports,* 27: 61-62, 1970.

Lester, D.: Sex differences in suicidal behavior. In Gomberg, E., & Frank, V. (Eds.) *Gender and disordered behavior: Sex differences in psychopathology.* New York: Brunner/Mazel, 1979.

Lester, D.: *Why people kill themselves,* (2nd ed.). Springfield, IL: Charles C Thomas, 1983.

Lester, D.: Suicide. In Widom, C. (Ed.), *Sex roles and psychopathology.* New York: Plenum, 1984.

Lester, D., & Reeve, C.: The suicide notes of young and old people. *Psychological Reports,* 50: 334, 1982.

Linehan, M.: Suicide and attempted suicide. *Perceptual and Motor Skills,* 37: 31-34, 1973.

McIntosh, J., & Jewell, B.: Sex difference trends in completed suicide. *Suicide and Life-Threatening Behavior,* 16: 16-27, 1986.

Maris, R.: *Pathways to suicide.* Baltimore, MD: The Johns Hopkins University Press, 1981.

Ornstein, M.: The impact of marital status, age and employment on female suicide in British Columbia. *Canadian Review of Sociology and Anthropology,* 20: 196-100, 1983.

Runyan, W.: In defense of the case study method. *American Journal of Orthopsychiatry,* 52: 440-446, 1982.

S.A.S. Institute Inc.: *SAS users guide: Statistics,* (5th ed.). Gary, N.C.: S.A.S. Institute Inc., 1985.

Shneidman, E.: *Voices of death.* New York: Harper & Row, 1980.

Shneidman, E.: *Definition of Suicide.* New York: Wiley, 1985.

Shneidman, E., & Farberow, N.: *Clues to suicide.* New York: McGraw-Hill, 1957.

Siegel, S.: *Nonparametric statistics.* New York: McGraw-Hill, 1956.

Stengel, E.: *Suicide and attempted suicide.* Baltimore, MD: Penguin, 1964.

Tomlinson-Keasey, C., Warren, L., & Elliot, J.: Suicide among gifted women: A prospective study. *Journal of Abnormal Psychology,* 95: 123-130, 1986.

Windelband, W.: *Geschichte und Naturwissenchaft.* Strassburg: Heitz, 1904.

Wolff, H.: Suicide notes. *American Mercury,* 24: 264-272, 1931.

APPENDIX

The protocol sentences which were derived from ten suicidologists' formulations regarding suicide, organized in significant clusters.

I-Unbearable Psychological Pain

1) In the suicide note, the person communicates flight from one of the following: pain, incurable disease, the threat of helpless senility, a violent death; from anticipated rejection or fear of becoming dependent; or self-depreciation, feelings of sexual or general inadequacy, humiliation, unknown danger. *However,* the suicide does not appear to be caused only by such a single thing; other motives (elements, wishes) appear to be evident (Menninger). P & D

The symbol — P— refers to a specific highly predictive variable, whereas the symbol — D — refers to a specific differentiating variable.

2) In the suicide note, the following emotional states are evident: pitiful forlornness, deprivation, distress and/or grief (Murray). P & D

3) In the suicide note, the person, who appears to have arrived at the end of his/her limited social interest, sees his/her suicide as a solution for an urgent problem and/or the injustices of life (Adler). P

4) In the suicide note, a clash is evident between a demand of adaptation and the individual's constitutional inability to meet the challenge (Jung). P

5) In the suicide note, it appears that although the suicide act does not have adaptive (survival) value, the suicide does have adjustive value for the individual. The suicide is functional because it abolishes painful tension for the individual; it provides relief from intolerable suffering (Murray). P

6) In the suicide note, the person is in a state of heightened disturbance (perturbation); e.g., he/she feels boxed in, rejected, harassed, unsuccessful, and especially hopeless and helpless (Shneidman). P

II–Interpersonal Relations

7) In the suicide note, unresolved problems in the individual are evident, where he/she has suffered defeat, at least for the time being and where there is something he/she cannot evade or overcome. His/Her weak spots in every sense of the word are evident (Jung). P

8) In the suicide note, the suicide appears to be related to unsatisfied or frustrated needs; e.g., achievement, affiliation, autonomy, dominance, etc., although it may be difficult to determine precisely which needs are operating at the time the note was written (Murray). P

9) In the suicide note, the communication allows one to conclude that the suicide appeared to be determined by the individual's history and the present interpersonal situation (Sullivan). P

10) In the suicide note, the person appears to be under stress of a situational factor which changes a relatively unvarying disturbance in interpersonal relations to one that is relatively persisting to a traumatic degree (Sullivan). P

11) In the suicide note, the person's communications indicate that his/her field of interpersonal relations are disturbed. A positive development in those same disturbed relations was held as the only possible way to go on living, but such development was seen as not forthcoming (Sullivan). P

12) In the suicide note, there is, direct or indirect evidence or inference of too great an attachment and too intimate (and primitive) a relationship, no matter how conventionally correct, of the suicide to any other person (e.g., family member) keeping him/her under the constant strain of having wishes (e.g., closeness, incestuous) stimulated and inhibited at one and the same time (Zilboorg). D

III–Rejection — Aggression

13) In the suicide note, the communications suggest that the person's personality (ego) organization is not adequately developed ("primitive", "weak") and narcissistic (Zilboorg). P & D

14) In the suicide note, it appears that the unconscious has created a situation in which death is desired, partly in order to hurt/attack someone else, or as an act of revenge towards someone who has slighted him/her. One can conclude that the person by attacking himself/herself is likely attacking another person (Adler). P

15) In the suicide note, the person communicates the existence of a traumatic event (e.g., an unmet love, a failing marriage, disgust with one's work) that results in a deep hurt, being desperate and ultimately the suicide itself (Jung). P

16) In the suicide note, although the person may not state this directly, there is evidence that a particular, significant other person(s), who was a destructive influence in the individual's past, is the target of the self-destruction. Self-destruction may not have been the only goal of the individual; the individual may well have calculated that the act would have a prolonged evil effect on this other person(s) (Sullivan). P

17) In the suicide note, the person communicates that he/she is preoccupied with a person that he/she had lost or who had rejected him/her (Freud). D

18) In the suicide note, the person communicates that he/she is feeling quite ambivalent; i.e., affectionate and hostile towards a lost or rejecting person (Freud). D

19) In the suicide note, the person communicates feelings and/or ideas of vengefulness and aggression towards himself/herself; however, he/she appears to be angry towards someone else (Freud). D

20) In the suicide note, the person communicates that he/she is turning back upon himself/herself murderous impulses that had been directed against someone else (Freud). D

IV–Inability to Adjust

21) In the suicide note, the individual considers himself/herself too weak to overcome his/her personal difficulties and therefore (in revenge) rejects everything with one full swoop in order to escape the feeling of inferiority, and/or to act intelligent according to his/her goal of coping with the difficulties of life (with disregard to the community—a beloved person, a teacher, society or the world at large) (Adler). P

22) In the suicide note, the person points out, with passionate eloquence and with flawless logic (from his/her perspective) that life is hard, bitter, futile and hopeless; that it entails more pain than pleasures; that there is no profit or purpose in it for him/her and no conceivable justification for living on (Menninger). P

23) In the suicide note, there is evidence of *one* of the following serious disorders of social behavior:

   (a) There is evidence consistent with the "down phase" of a manic-depressive disorder. For example, there is a sort of all-embracing (grandiose) negative self appraisal—he/she is no good, has never been any good, and has caused everyone else a great deal of trouble, which can only be ended by destroying onself.

   (b) There is evidence consistent with a diagnosis of schizophrenia. For example, the schizophrenic ends his/her life quite incidentally to some fantastic procedure for the remedy of his/her distress: to be reborn, to protect others from some delusional contamination, to save the world, to demonstrate omnipotence and the like.

   (c) There is evidence consistent with the diagnosis of obsessive-compulsive disorder. For example, the individual exhibits obsessional characteristics such as overwhelming suicidal thoughts with unlimited attention to the detail of such an act.

   (d) There is evidence consistent with a diagnosis of psychopathic disorder. For example, the note is a tool for ensuring attention of others, but the act itself was likely an accidental misjudgement—too great a dose of poison, too long a delay in calling for help, and so forth.

   (e) There is evidence consistent with a diagnosis of depressive disorder. For example, the person exhibits a "reverie" of self-depreciating statements and appears to be very restrictive in thoughts and actions.

(f) There is no evidence of a serious specific disorder but the note appears to be written by an individual who is so baffled in his/her attempt to subjugate his/her interests, that a paralysis of interest in others and in future possibilities of self has progressed to the point that life has become colorless and completely wholly unattractive (Sullivan). P

V–Indirect Expressions

24) In the suicide note, the person communicates ambivalence; e.g., complications, concomitant contradictory feelings, attitudes and/or thrusts (Shneidman). P & D
25) In the suicide note, the individual's aggression appears to have been turned inward. Themes of humility, submission and devotion, subordination, flagelation or masochism are evident (Adler). P
26) In the suicide note, the person's communications appear to have unconscious psychodynamic implications (Shneidman). D

VI–Identification — Egression

27) In the suicide note, there is evidence for egression (defined as a person's intended departure from a region of distress, chiefly with the aim of terminating, with relief, of the pain he/she has been suffering) and desertion (e.g., from the suicide's closest bonded person) (Murray). P
28) In the suicide note, the person communicates that he/she is in some direct or indirect fashion identifying with a rejecting or lost person (Freud). D
29) In the suicide note, an unwillingness to accept sickness, old age or too many painful emotions, not only made it possible for the suicide to accept death willingly, even to seek it, but it also generally led him/her to project his/her ideal beyond life (e.g., hereafter) where life is eternal and forever devoid of any discomfort (Zilboorg). D

VII–Ego

30) In the suicide note, a "complex" is evident, i.e., something discordant, unassimilated and antagonistic exists (e.g., symptoms, ideas), perhaps as an obstacle, pointing to unresolved problems in the individual (Jung). P
31) In the suicide note, the person communicates that his/her suicide is a fulfillment of punishment, i.e., self-punishment (Freud). D

32) In the suicide note, the communications indicate that the person wishes to die; i.e., the suicide is accomplished due to some relative weakness in the capacity for developing constructive tendencies (e.g., attachment, love) (Menninger). D

VIII–Cognitive Constriction

33) In the suicide note, the person communicates evidence of adult trauma (e.g., poor health, rejection by the spouse, being married to a competing spouse) (Shneidman). P & D

34) In the suicide note, the person appears to be figuratively intoxicated or drugged by one's overpowering emotions and constricted logic and perception (Shneidman). D

35) In the suicide note, there is a poverty of thought, exhibited by the individual expressing only permutations and combinations of grief-provoking content (Sullivan). D

Unassigned Variable

36) In the suicide note, the communications indicate that the suicide is a primitive and impulsive and semi-ceremonial outcome more of frustrated closeness wishes than of aggressive wishes or of spite (Zilboorg). D

CHAPTER 7

THE SOCIAL RELATIONSHIPS
OF SUICIDAL WOMEN

B. JOYCE STEPHENS

TWO PATTERNS in the phenomenon of suicide attempting have been well-documented in the literature: a skewed distribution along sex lines and the interpersonal nature of such behaviors. For most of the western world, attempting suicide is primarily a female behavior and the precipitating factors typically involve severe, often chronic interpersonal conflicts with significant others. It is therefore surprising that despite the prevalence of published studies which emphasize the role of conflict in the social relationships of suicidal women, there has been a general failure to pinpoint and describe the specific forms these conflicts assume.

We know, for example, that suicidal women often experience multiple stresses in their relationships with their spouses or boyfriends, yet the discussions of these interactions and their dynamics have tended to be vague and general. Similarly, researchers have noted the importance of early childhood relationships in the onset of depression and suicidal ideation, but there is a paucity of systematic treatment of family variables. Particularly lacking are studies of the suicidal individuals' viewpoints on their family interactions and experiences. This is doubly perplexing when we consider that at least one major theory of the genesis of suicidal behaviors links these acts to defects in personality development arising out of pathological parent-child relationships.

If suicidologists agree on one thing, it is that ultimately suicidal behaviors are not understandable as specific acts but are rather possible outcomes of more general social processes which precede the act and provide a matrix from which self-destructive attitudes and roles may arise. Viewing suicide attempting as processual in nature, it becomes necessary not only to identify those patterns of interactions which foster personal despair and self-hatred but also to trace these patterns developmentally. The present study reports on the findings of a group of female suicide attempters and traces how these women have accumulated interpersonal histories of frustration and self-damage in their relationships with others. Three developmental periods and how they build on one another are described—childhood family relationships, relationships during adolescence, and adult relationships with males.

METHODOLOGY

The life histories of fifty adult female suicide attempters were obtained through taped interviews by the researcher. Personal documents (diaries, letters, etc.) of the subjects were also analyzed and additional materials collected by interviews with the subjects' therapists (in those cases where the individual was in therapy) and by the researcher's weekly attendance at group counselling sessions with the subjects.

The women ranged in age from eighteen to sixty-three, with a median age of thirty-four. All of the women were Caucasian (one subject was Hispanic). All income levels were represented. Four of the subjects had a grade school education, thirty-three had completed high school, and thirteen had completed or were completing college. Twenty-eight were housewives, sixteen were employed full-time, and six were students. Sixteen of the women were never married, fifteen were married, five were separated from their spouses, and fourteen were divorced.

Twenty-seven subjects had made a single suicide attempt and twenty-three had made more than one attempt. The multiple attempters had made an average of 2.8 attempts. Thirty-one subjects had used poisoning, ten had combined methods, seven had used cutting instruments, and two had used firearms. Several of the subjects had engaged in acts of an ambiguously suicidal character, but only those deliberate acts of self-injury in which the individual expressed the intent to die and which necessitated emergency medical treatment were considered to be suicide attempts in this study.

FINDINGS

A. Childhood Family Relationships

Five major themes characterized the parent-child relationships of these women; non-nurturing parents, absent parents, abusive parents, mentally ill parents, and alcoholic parents. As children, the subjects grew up in home environments which were instrumental in shaping their low self-esteem and feelings of chronic insecurity. As role models, their families impressed upon them the unreliability of relationships and the punishing consequences of relationships.

The most common pattern of parent-child relationships was lack of nurturance and emotional neglect. In some cases actual abandonment of the subject had occurred. The women described their families as not expressing affection and relentlessly critical of them; unhappiness and fear were a "normal" condition of their childhood. Many of them believed and still believe that their parents did not love them or want to care for them.

They reported early feelings of depression that resulted from their belief that they were rejected and unloved by their parents. Few reported close relationships with their siblings or other family members. As children, they were uncertain, insecure, and reluctant to attempt other relationships. All were socially isolated with few relationships outside the family. In most cases their inability to form new relationships grew directly out of their parents' disregard for them which they quickly translated into feelings of worthlessness.

The subjects described their parents as critical and punishing. As children and now as adults, they have had to wage an ongoing battle to define themselves as worthwhile and lovable. But their efforts to bolster self-esteem are compromised by these early experiences which negated self-worth.

They saw their parents as manipulative and combining rejection with impossible demands for perfection. Failure to measure up to their parents' expectations was met with punishment that ranged from withdrawal of love to physical beatings. When one subject as a child displeased her mother, she was made to parade through the neighborhood shouting out her misdeed and promising never to do it again. Several of the subjects remember, with a resentment that has not abated, a family theme of "be perfect" which was directed at them.

Nearly a third of the subjects had not grown up in intact homes with both parents present. In nine cases the parents had divorced, in five cases a parent had died, in three cases a parent had been committed to a state institution, and in three cases the subjects grew up in foster homes. The women retained vivid memories of the harmful effects of these losses and attributed in varying degrees their own unhappy childhoods to the loss of their parents.

The most striking cases were those in which the subjects had been put in foster care. They were careful to point out that finances had not motivated the action and interpreted it as the decisions of uncaring and even vicious parents. Not atypically, they experienced their parents' actions as punishment. Although the subjects who were reared in foster homes represent an extreme, they share in common with the other subjects, whose childhoods were marred by absent parents, lasting feelings of resentment and rejection. The subjects, sometimes unreasonably, continue to blame their families and at the same time search for some defect in themselves to explain what happened to them.

Thirty percent of the subjects had been physically and/or sexually abused by their families. The physical abuse ranged from sporadic and unpredictable acts of violence to frequent, severe beatings. In many cases the abusive parent was also an alcoholic. As children, the subjects feared their parents and tended to withdraw into passivity and depression. None could recall having another family member intercede for them. Lacking any aid, they adopted strategies of exaggerated docility to please the parent and escape the physical violence.

The betrayal implicit in the sexual exploitation of children endures as an unresolved conflict for those subjects whose childhood involved sexual assault and incest. This conflict assumes the pernicious form of self-blame and guilt for rarely do the subjects express anger toward the offender, rather they feel confused and sympathetic and make attempts to rationalize the behavior of the family member. One woman, for example, whose father had committed incest with her sister and attempted it with her, blamed not her father but herself and her mother. In two cases, the subjects were raped, one by her uncle and the other by her mother's live-in boyfriend. Both subjects now "hate" men and sex and have been unable to establish close relationships with males.

Over a quarter of the women had at least one family member who had been diagnosed as suffering from mental illness. Clinical depression, schizophrenia, and alcoholism headed the list. Unfortunately, many of the subjects fear that they may be "tainted," having somehow inherited mental illness and they partially attribute their suicidal tendencies to a hypothetical family trait. Usually, the subjects became aware that something was "not right" in their family at an early age but were unable to understand what it was and their confusion was compounded by their families' attempts to cover up the problem.

In general, the subjects are intolerant and unforgiving of their parents' condition, holding the parents' illness responsible for their own unhappiness and suicidal tendencies. Paradoxically, they can forgive parents who sexually assaulted them but not parents exhibiting symptoms which they fear are connected with their own depressive states and suicidal behaviors.

Another quarter of the subjects had childhoods dominated by the alcoholism of one or both of their parents. As children, these subjects were intensely lonely and fearful; they described parents who themselves had so many problems as to have few resources left to be adequate parents. These subjects frequently became surrogate parents to their siblings and in some cases even to their hapless parents. Some of them fled from their disorganized home situation into early marriages; all of them were and are emotionally damaged. They associate their current problems with the failures and psychological deficits of their families-of-origin. They trace their depression to the misery which began when they realized that their families and by extension *they* were different from other families. Many are haunted by fears of their own adequacy to be good parents to *their* children.

For the women in this study, the multiple pathologies which characterized their childhood relationships have remained real and potent forces in their progression toward overt suicidal acts. For them, these sad early lessons about the nature of intimate relationships — they involve betrayal, neglect, abuse, and the engendering of feelings of worthlessness — are powerfully linked with their slide into depression and suicide attempting.

B. Relationships During Adolescence

The adolescence of the women was instrumental in the further promotion of feelings of worthlessness and hopelessness as relationships with their families and peers contributed to a diminishing sense of self-worth. Their socialization into roles which mitigated against the ability to perceive themselves as competent and effective human beings resulted in interpersonal experiences whose legacy was an enduring sense of failure and self-mortification.

Uniformly the subjects described their adolescence as an unhappy time which they would not want to relive. Their home environments were filled with conflict and tension between family members that frequently erupted into overt hostility and aggression. Typical adjectives they used to describe their parents were "critical," "punishing," "rejecting," "neglectful," "abusive," "manipulative," "cold," "disapproving."

All of the women recalled that as teenagers they felt isolated from family and friends, and "different" from their peers. Many of them carried the lack of self-esteem and feelings of insecurity in relationships into school, performing poorly and intensifying the aura of failure that permeated their lives. Some became overachievers but parental approval and self approval were not forthcoming. Relationships with peers and boyfriends mirrored the unhappy family constellation and provided no alternate source of self-worth. One legacy of their adolescence which accompanied them into adulthood was a psychologically disabling sense of their inability to form and maintain satisfying relationships with others.

Although all of the subjects experienced similar feelings of guilt, anger, and depression, their responses differed considerably. The terms "Cheap Thrills" and "Humble Pie" are expressive of the characteristics of two disparate patterns of adaptation by these subjects to the interpersonal problems of their adolescence. Superficially different, they are at their core, driven by the same fundamental pathologies in the social relationships of these girls.

Humble Pie was a pattern of over-conformity, docility and passivity in which the subjects assumed a guilty responsibility for the conflicts that surrounded them, and sought to appease and please others. They attempted, in short to be "good girls," even perfect girls. Cheap Thrills, on the other hand, was a pattern of defiance expressed in rebelliousness and other acting-out behaviors. These subjects transformed their depression and guilt into rage and tried to strike out at the interpersonal environment which had denied them any avenues to self-worth. They tried, with a vengeance, to be "bad girls."

The radically different adolescent patterns of Cheap Thrills and Humble Pie were accompanied by dissimilarities in social class background and subsequent suicidal careers. Subjects in the Cheap Thrills category were more likely to come from working class homes whereas the Humble Pie included more girls from middle class backgrounds. This association probably reflects class-based tolerance of female acting-out behaviors, i.e., middle class families exert more restraints on adolescent females than working class families do. The average age at the first suicide attempt also varied — 21.7 years for the Cheap Thrills girls and 29 years for the Humble Pie group. The "bad girls" were, surprisingly, less likely than the "good girls" to become multiple attempters and the latter were more likely to use violent methods than the former. These findings suggest that the suppressed rage of the Humble Pie girls, denied expression during adolescence, surfaced in even more self-destructive behaviors during their adulthood.

The Humble Pie girls were so overwhelmed by the conflicts around them that they became emotionally submerged in their families' problems. The failures of their families became *their* failures. Twin themes of failure and guilt are prominent in the adolescence of this group of subjects. It is as if they held on to the belief that if they were very good and constantly attentive to their families, they could somehow hold together the disintegrating relationships. For some, the burden became too heavy and they abandoned the role of family peacemaker and withdrew into themselves. Several of the girls were anorexic during this time and three of the subjects began self-mutilating in bizzare efforts to expiate their perceived shortcomings. As a group, they tended to be compulsive in their rigid adherence to rules; they seldom questioned or challenged the demands of authority figures. Although they resented the failure built into such situations, they could or would not express their resentment except as shame and depression.

Retreat into physical illness and dependency characterized the response of many of these subjects. One subject so successfully feigned illness that her parents withdrew her from high school for a year. All of the subjects who were either genuinely ill or feigned illness realized that these were strategies designed to remove them from what had become unbearable situations (school, peer groups, etc.). Further, they understood that these were also attempts to elicit some evidence of affection and succorance from their families.

In summarizing the adolescence of this group of subjects, one is struck by the almost martyr-like role they assumed, the extreme measures they were willing to take to please and protect their families, the submergence of their own needs and rights. They depart radically from stereotypical views of irresponsible teenagers; indeed, they may have been in many cases the most responsible member of their families. They carried the multiple burdens of families whose internal organization was severely compromised and whose members were unable to relate to each other in satisfying, ego-enhancing ways. One is also struck by the self-effacing quality of their behavior and their naive belief that by being "good," the affection and security so lacking in their lives would materialize. But their efforts were doomed as their families played out their tragic scenarios.

For the Cheap Thrills adaptation, rage and a desire to strike back at those whom they believed to be the causes of their unhappiness dominated adolescence. These subjects described themselves as "wild" and "unmanageable" during their teenage years, as frequently running away from home, using drugs, engaging in sexual escapades that in several cases resulted in pregnancy. Generally, they did poorly in school, had few friends, and had violent (sometimes physical) confrontations with both other family members and their peers. Unlike the depressed "good girls," these girls became angry "bad girls." They reacted aggressively to their painful feelings of being different from others and rejected by their families; they raised hell and caused trouble for everyone.

These girls did not assume responsibility for their families' problems but fought back bitterly in ways that were unfortunately often self-destructive. The disorganized nature of their family situations was paralleled in their own life-styles which focused on a continual search for excitement and stimulation. But life in the fast lane did not compensate for the emotional impoverishment of girls who grew up feeling hated and hateful, who were called "dumb," "ugly," "sick," "bad" by others. Although they exhibited an early pattern of multiple involvements in relationships outside the family, these relationships were markedly shallow and could do little to alleviate their isolation and hatred. Discord was a constant in their relationships with their many boyfriends, interactions punctuated by physical abuse which by now they had come to associate with intimacy.

Their penchant for making themselves troublesome led to a high proportion of these girls being taken by their parents to clinics and counselors. However there was seldom any follow-through and the parents rejected suggestions that they themselves ought to be in treatment. Consequently, the various acting-out behaviors of the subjects were defined as symptoms of their adjustment failures and having been labeled "bad" and presented with this role to play, they embraced it with a vengeance.

Both adaptive strategies, Cheap Thrills and Humble Pie, proved in the long run to be dysfunctional. Docility failed and rebellion failed, neither being sufficient to compensate for the lack of self-enhancing experiences in their relationships with significant others. Depressed and hostile as teenagers, they became depressed and suicidal as adults.

C. Adult Relationships with Males

Four major themes dominated the relationships of these women with their men — "smothering love," infidelity, battering, and denial of affection. All of the women expressed deep unhappiness in their experiences with adult males and the typical picture was one of dysfunctional patterns which had lasted for years. For many of them, the suicide attempt represented simultaneously a flight from the unhappy relationship and a desperate effort to restore it on a different footing.

The suicidal careers of ten of the women were facilitated by what can only be described as unrealistic expectations of the love relationship. These subjects had a consuming investment in their relationships with their partners. They described themselves as unable to exist without their partners, as needing the relationship in order to continue, and as incapable of imagining themselves without their partners. Constantly demanding proof of their partners' love and affection, they sought to establish relationships with men in which all of their emotional needs would be met. Needless to say, they met with disappointment. As their own self-worth existed only in terms of unremitting attention and devotion from their men, any flagging of attention was immediately interpreted by them as emotional abandonment and plunged them into despair. The center of their lives was their partner and they required that he reciprocate. For them, there could be no meaningful existence outside of the relationship.

They viewed any activity or interest in which they were not included as failure by their partner to meet their needs, and it is likely that their quest for a smothering love had been instrumental in the high incidence of break-ups which characterized their relationships with men. In nearly all the cases, the men had either gradually withdrawn from or abruptly fled the relationship. Even those women who had children or pursued careers outside the home downplayed the importance of these roles and oriented themselves singlemindedly toward their partners. They held very traditional values about the primacy of males and insisted that along with being the protector, breadwinner, and lover, their partner should carry the major responsibility for securing their happiness and self-esteem.

Many of the women were quite articulate in expressing themselves and the sole topic of their verbalizations concerned their feelings and emotional needs. They were rather overwhelming in their relentless pursuit of and endless analysis of the state of their emotional fulfillment. At times, one could not help but empathize with their partners' efforts to escape such emotional dependency. The men were shadowy figures in the scenarios that these subjects unfolded. Whether this was due to a tendency of the women to be drawn to emotionally cool men who in fact neglected them or whether this was due to the womens' exclusive preoccupation with themselves is not clear. What is clear is that for these women identity and self-worth were hinged on a particular kind of relationship that had not been achieved.

In a majority of the cases, sexual infidelity by the spouse or boyfriend had severely aggravated an already strained relationship and precipitated the suicide attempt. The subjects were explicit in linking the infidelity to their suicide attempts. Two disparate patterns characterized their partners' sexual betrayal; in the first, the partner had been involved with a procession of other women over the years and the subjects' suicide attempts were the culmination of their despair over the situation. In the second pattern, the subjects' suicide attempts were reactions to a single, atypical infidelity by the partner. The first pattern was the more common.

Frequently the partners' infidelities were combined with almost nightly absences from the home. Over time the subjects were unable to find any security in such a situation and increasingly found themselves unable to cope with the deteriorating relationship. In two cases the women had tolerated their partners' infidelities until they discovered that their own teenage daughters had been sexually involved with the men. Both women attempted suicide shortly after discovering this and one subsequently left her husband. In three cases the subject attempted suicide upon learning that her partner had fathered children with other women.

All of the women had made repeated efforts to work out the problem with their partners but in not one case did they report receiving cooperation from their partners. Rather, they were met with more lies and avoidance. For those women who had left their partners, both the suicide attempt and the break-up of the relationship were largely consequences of the partners' infidelity. The women who continued to have intimate contact with philandering partners expressed strong dissatisfaction with the relationships.

At the time of the suicide attempt, twelve subjects were in relationships with men which exposed them to physical abuse. The degrees and instances of battering included slapping, choking, hitting with closed fists, threats with firearms, and ranged from occasionally to frequently. In several of the cases the physical aggression was associated with a partners' drug or alcohol abuse.

All but one of the subjects were reluctant to talk about the violence in their relationships and expressed varying amounts of embarrassment and shame over the battering episodes. As the subjects were generally inclined to downplay the instances of violence and only those women who had been actually physically assaulted by their partners were included in this category, it is probable that the actual frequency of abuse was higher.

Usually the women blamed themselves for the attacks and made excuses for their men, a pattern well known to researchers of domestic violence. Also, they voiced fear of their partners and commonly felt that there was no one to whom they could talk about the violence in their lives. Several women described feeling like prisoners in their relationships with their violent partners. In some of the cases, battering not only preceded the suicide attempt of the subject but also followed it. When one of the subjects tried to overdose on a bottle of pain pills, her husband beat her severely and threatened to kill her if she ever did anything like that again. Another subject was hit and choked by her husband when he discovered her suicide attempt. Tellingly, these women described their suicide attempts as a way of escaping from a brutal relationship and as a way of having revenge.

The most common theme characterizing their relationships with males was what the women described as uncaring and emotionally indifferent partners. Two-thirds of the subjects described their partners as unwilling to express even rudimentary affection for them or other family members. As one of the women put it: "My husband is a cold, a very, very, very cold person. He's not the type of man to do things with the family. He has nothing to do with the family. He doesn't enjoy us, he suffers us." Often the subjects reacted to their partners' lack of emotional involvement by seeking outside help. Most of them had been in some form of counselling with the hope of working out their difficulties; unfortunately, when they attempted to involve their partners in therapy, they were met with ridicule, resistance, and even hostility. Many of their men countered with the argument that since *they* were unhappy, then *they* needed help. The partners actively rejected the idea that they might have played a role in the womens' deepening depression and cited the depressive state as proof of the womens' responsibility for the sad state of the relationships. At the time of this study, many of the subjects had given up on efforts to enlist their partners' cooperation in seeking professional help (not a single partner was in therapy, some had gone once or twice then stopped).

Unlike the women discussed earlier whose unrealistic emotional demands had alienated their partners, these women were not trying to get their partners in emotional strangleholds. They recognized that their relationships were onesided investments from which their partners extracted much but paid in little. Eventually, the rationalizations that these women had relied upon to explain to themselves their partners' lack of feeling and care (alcohol, drugs, "other women," immaturity, etc.) failed to restore the relationships to any footing which could shore up their dwindling sense of self. As failure and negation had dominated their other relationships with the significant people in their lives, so too the commonality which all of these women share—their low self-esteem, feelings of powerlessness and worthlessness—was exacerbated in their intimate relationships with men.

The chronic tensions these women experienced in their relationships with their husbands, boyfriends, and lovers acted as precipitating factors in their suicide attempts. These are unhappy, even pathological interactions in which the women are unloved, beaten and brutalized, sexually betrayed, and inevitably they sink deeper into the morass that has become their lives. The ultimately devastating consequences of being in loveless and emotionally barren relationships accelerate the suicidal process.

Conclusion

All of the women in this study had interpersonal histories of relentlessly negative relationships with the most important people in their lives—their mothers and fathers, their peers, their spouses and lovers. Their social and psychological experiences have prepared them to be victims, victims of parents, of men, of relationships in which the self is continually mortified. Their self-denigrating experiences begin early in life, continue in their adulthood, are incessant and self-perpetuating.

Their careers in self-destruction began early within family systems which generated fear and unhappiness as a "normal" condition of their childhood. Many of them were physically abused by other family members and none of them grew up in homes which could be described as nuturing or loving. Their home environments provided fertile ground for the development of chronic feelings of inadequacy and futility. From these pathological family systems they learned that relationships mean betrayal and pain.

They frequently asserted that they were "bad" and wished to be "normal." As children, they became convinced that they were different from other children and even though they now understand, at least in part, that they were the victims of their parents, they hold on to the idea that they were in some way responsible for their families' problems. Their desires to become "normal" are tragic echoes of childhoods characterized by disorganization and neglect. They cannot relive their childhood; their childhood can never be made "normal." Yet, they continue to rehearse their early experiences in their adult relationships.

During their adolescence, they adopted the interpersonal strategies of Humble Pie and Cheap Thrills to cope with what they perceived as an implacably hostile world. The submissiveness of the Humble Pie girls reflected their lack of appreciation of their own individuality, which later was played out in deliberate acts to destroy their damaged selves. When talking with these subjects, one was never sure that they understood their own separateness; their "selves" were like borrowed clothes they did not own which eventually must be returned to the rightful owners.

The open warfare strategy of Cheap Thrills could hardly be considered a healthier strategy as inevitably it brought the individuals into direct conflict with their tormentors. The effort to break out of the victim role failed at generating self-esteem and, indeed, merely provided more victimizing experiences. For both Humble Pie and Cheap Thrills girls, the victim role became increasingly more stabilized and nowhere is this more apparent than in their relationships with men.

The price of intimacy is very high for these women, entailing physical abuse, sexual betrayal, emotional impoverishment, and self-negation. They are continually reminded of their own worthlessness by the hostile and punishing interactions they seem unable to avoid. Both the continuation and the destruction of these relationships are directly implicated in their suicide attempts.

The final stage, when they become overtly suicidal, is the culmination of all that has come before. As one woman expressed it: "All my life I've felt like nothing, nothing, just nothing." Her words embody the suicidal process in women — women who have learned from their relationships that they are nothing, just nothing.

REFERENCES

This chapter is based on research reported in the following articles:

Stephens, B. J.: Suicidal women and their relationships with their parents. *Omega*, 16: 289-300, 1985-1986.

Stephens, B. J.: Cheap thrills and humble pie. *Suicide & Life-Threatening Behavior*, 17: 107-118, 1987.

Stephens, B. J.: Suicidal women and their relationships with husbands, boyfriends, and lovers. *Suicide & Life-Threatening Behavior*, 15: 77-90, 1985.

CHAPTER 8

AMBIGUITY IN THE INTERPRETATION OF SUICIDE: FEMALE DEATH IN PAPUA, NEW GUINEA

DOROTHY AYERS COUNTS[1]

Shamed and angry, Galiki grated oil from a plant called Navue and asked her grandmother to rub it on her body. When she was anointed and dressed in her finery, she took her turtle shell bracelets and broke them. Then she put her hands and feet in the ashes of her fire as a sign that she expected to die.

THIS SCENE from a West New Britain folktale describes the emotions and actions of a young woman who, forced by her parents into an unwanted marriage with a disgusting and only semi-human man, prepares herself for death. Her preparations—dressing in her finery, destruction of her treasured possessions and covering herself with the ashes of a dead fire—are the ritualized behaviors that are associated with suicide when it functions as a form of social control (see Giddens 1964:115 for a discussion of this point).

In this chapter I will discuss suicide, especially female suicide, as a culturally recognized behavior that acts as a form of social sanction among the people of West New Britain Province, Papua New Guinea. It is, and I argue it is intended to be, an act that has political consequences both for the surviving kin and for those who are held responsible for the events that lead to the death. Then I will turn to a more problematic situation: the interpretation of self-killing when the act violates cultural expectations—when the appropriate rituals are not followed, rendering the meaning of the suicide unclear and the cultural message ambiguous. The interpretation that others place on the circumstances surrounding an ambiguous death is, I argue, based on their prior relationship to the deceased and/or to the culpable individuals rather than on relevant facts in the case. Indeed, when they discuss the death, the survivors may expand on or ignore events in order to strengthen a particular explanation for it, or interpretation of its meaning. I will illustrate with cases of ambiguous and unambiguous suicide that occurred in the Kaliai area of West New Britain in 1975, 1979, and 1985.

Suicide as a culturally recognized form of behavior is widely reported in Melanesia. Hoskin, Friedman, and Cawte say that for Arawe children of southwest New Britain, " . . . suicide is part of the child's concept of his world." They describe a game in which suicide was part of children's play (1969:206):

> The oldest of the children, an 8 year-old girl, suggested that a man might have hanged himself. She ran to a banana palm, loosely tied a hanging dead branch around her neck, inverted her eyelids, knotted her fingers, and dropped limply to the ground. She then jumped to her feet and the other two ran squealing in mock terror. Next it was their turn to . . . hang themselves and chase everyone.

Healey indicates that the Maring of the Bismarck Mountains of New Guinea recognize a "range of socially acceptable and recognizable underlying factors that may precipitate suicide" (1979:95), while Berndt comments that "in certain circumstances the Fore of New Guinea regard suicide "as the 'right' course of action" (1962:181). Furthermore, suicide is part of the oral tradition of the Lusi-Kaliai of West New Britain (Counts 1980, 1984, 1987), the people of East Kwaio, Malaita (Akin 1985), the Kwara'ae of Malaita (Gegeo and Watson-Gegeo 1985), and the Bimin-Kuskusmin of Papua New Guinea (Poole 1985), among others.

One widespread culturally recognized condition that results in suicide is the shame of the powerless person. McKellin observes that among the Managalase of Oro Province, Papua New Guinea (1985:9):

> The shame that produces suicide arises when an individual does not believe him or herself to be at fault, but is also not able to demonstrate innocence to his or her peers.

As a response to shame, suicide may be a form of social sanction used by victims to take revenge on those who have humiliated them: it may be the "revenge suicide" described by Jeffreys (1952). Although it is not universally the case (see, for example, Marshall 1979 and Poole 1985 for discussions of male suicide), the powerless persons who resort to suicide as a way of punishing others are frequently women. Sivers reports that suicide among the Aguaruna Jivaro of Peru is a "normal act of punishment" and recounts a case in which a man was accused of murder, arrested, and jailed after a girl whom he had refused to marry killed herself (1982:6). The suicide of Aguaruna women is "at once a response to a stressful social role, a means of asserting some degree of control or autonomy, and, when suicide is actually accomplished, a means of avenging oneself by inflicting harm on one's tormentor" (Brown 1982:8). Brown concludes, however, that suicide is defective as an instrument of power because "it reproduces the very social and symbolic structures that make self-destruction a compelling option" (Brown 1986:326). He goes on to say (ibid.):

> When women translate their anger into suicidal acts, they demonstrate their social impotence, thereby confirming men's prejudices and contributing to the reproduction of the social meanings that make suicide attractive in the first place. Worse still, the current high frequency of suicide among Aguaruna women tends to vitiate the coercive power of suicide threats because men can no longer see a clear connection between their own behavior and the suicidal behavior of women. "It doesn't matter how you treat your wife," one bewildered man told me. "Women now just kill themselves for no reason."

In Papua New Guinea, suicide may be a way of escaping from social relationships that women consider to be intolerable, as Reay reports is true of Kuma women (1959), or it may have a more explicit component of revenge as with the Huli response described by Frankel (1986). Berndt reports that suicide may be an aggressive response to humiliation that allows a Fore to inflict harm and injury on an offender (1962:204). A married Fore woman, for example, has no legal rights in her husband's village, and because she can expect her kinsmen to avenge her, suicide may be the most effective way that a wronged wife can injure her husband. Suicide also seems to have an aspect of revenge among the people of Mount Hagen. Marilyn Strathern (1972:281-283) notes that a Mount Hagen woman may kill herself as a result of shame or in a state of *popokl* or "revenge-anger." As Andrew Strathern observes, the concept of *popokl* " . . . points out the guilt and hence the responsibility of others in relation to a harmed person" (1975:351). In his detailed case study of the suicide of a Maring woman, Healey views suicide as the "act of a woman who has unilaterally assumed a transcendent power, above that accorded her by her inferior status . . . " and examines the consequences of her act for her survivors (1979:94), while Johnson, following Jeffreys (1951), interprets female suicide among the

Gainj as "samsonic" or revenge suicide (Johnson 1981:332). Johnson portrays Gainj women as consistent losers in the contest of relations between the sexes that have become "an analog of war" (ibid.:328). They are hard working, malnourished, almost always either pregnant or lactating during their reproductive lives, and they are "protected, managed, and controlled" by men. Gainj wives kill themselves when their husbands fail to give them the support and protection that they consider to be their right: specifically a Gainj woman's suicide is the result either of public physical abuse by her husband or of his refusal to support her in her fight with another woman, usually a co-wife. Her suicide has too consequences: it removes a woman from an intolerable situation and it visits lasting revenge on her husband. Because the Gainj believe in the ability of malevolent ghosts to inflict harm, her death renders her husband vulnerable to supernatural attack and also thoroughly humiliates him. Says Johnson (ibid.:332):

> Thus the husband of a suicide loses assets—his wife, the brideprice he paid for her and the compensation he now must pay [to her angry kin], and status. He is a man who has been thoroughly and publicly bested by a woman. Suicide is a drastic, a final, but a magnificently autonomous act; it leaves no doubt as to who controls one's life.

According to Frankel, Huli women who are beaten by their husbands may either mutilate themselves or commit suicide. He observes that "a woman's suicide is a serious blow to her husband's clan if it appears from his ill-treatment. He is held as responsible as if he had murdered her. Where women's means of gaining redress are limited, suicide represents a desperate means of retribution, for they can be confident that major compensation will be given. . . ." (Frankel 1986:135).

The Maenge of New Britain do not consider suicide to be proper behavior for everyone; rather it " . . . is a type of death appropriate only to 'rubbish men' and 'women' (Panoff 1977:50). In his analysis of the types of social persons who are inclined to kill themselves among the Maenge, Panoff reports that suicide occurs primarily among two categories of people: orphans and women—" . . . precisely those [categories] whose members have the fewest opportunities to pour out their aggressiveness" (1977:55). He concludes that the suicides committed by Maenge women and by "men of silence" or "rubbish men" belong to Jeffreys's category of samsonic suicide.

Let us turn now to an examination of the way that the people of Kaliai interpret suicide and the results of death by one's own hand.

THE LUSI OF KALIAI

Kaliai is a political district in West New Britain Province, Papua, New Guinea. The Lusi-speaking Kaliai people who are the subject of this chapter number about one thousand and live in five villages and a number of small hamlets along the northwest New Britain coast. They are normatively patrilineal and patrivirilocal and have no ranked hierarchy and no inherited office. Differential access to authority and power exist on the basis of age, sex, birth order, and personality. That is to say, everything else being equal, an older first-born male has an advantage over his younger siblings and a husband has authority over his wife. An aggressive, strong-willed first-born woman is, however, a force to be reckoned with — a subject that I will return to. In spite of the inherent power advantage enjoyed by older or first-born males, there are a number of factors that serve to prevent the unrestrained enjoyment of that power.

First, there are supernatural sanctions against the abuse of power: the punishment by angry, avenging ancestral spirits of villagers who neglect and abuse the helpless is a recurrent theme in oral literature. During the celebration of mortuary rituals and rites for first-born children, masked figures representing the ancestors dance and choruses of men sing songs that, according to legend, were taught by ancestor spirits to orphans, reminding villagers of their obligation to care for the helpless and the needy and of the dire consequences of the irresponsible exercise of power.

Second, a person may appeal to the national code of law as a source of authority to support her position if she feels that her rights are being abrogated, as was successfully done during a moot described in detail in Counts and Counts (1974). Also, an abused woman may successfully take her husband to court. New Britain courts do levy substantial fines on men who beat their wives with sticks or other implements rather than merely with their hands. Wife beating that is not continuous, that does not expose the woman's genitals or otherwise shame her or her relatives, and that does not involve the use of other than a man's hand seems to be an aspect of marriage that is accepted as normal by both women and men.

Third, a person may appeal to her kinsmen for help against a more powerful person. This is especially important for married women, for a woman's ties to her natal group continue throughout her life. She maintains an especially close relationship with her brother, supporting him by contributing wealth and food to ceremonies that he sponsors while he contributes to the bridewealth for her sons, her children inherit coconut palms from him, and he comes to her assistance if she is severely beaten or humiliated by her husband. In this case, he will likely either intervene to stop the mistreatment or sound the bullroarer as a public expression of his anger and grief, and of the displeasure of the ancestors at the mistreatment of his kinswoman. In turn, the husband must distribute gifts of shell money and pork to his wife's kin (but not to her) to mollify them, and he knows that further abuse of his wife will likely lead to violent conflict with them. A woman whose kin live in a distant village is at a severe disadvantage if she has an abusive husband, for her kin and life-long acquaintances are unlikely to be willing to offend him in order to defend her, even if they consider his treatment of her to be unnecessarily harsh.

Fourth, a woman may look to her female kin for support. Although I know of no case in which a woman publicly supported her sister or daughter against her male kin, women quietly attempt to influence their male relatives and occasionally they conspire to defy them. This is especially the case if a father arranges the marriage of his daughter without consulting her or considering her wishes, as is his right to do. A loving father tries to select a man who is acceptable to his daughter, but the promotion of his interests and prestige, and that of his sons, is his first concern, and if his daughter's wishes conflict with his interest, male priorities take precedence. My data strongly suggest that this ideal has never been enthusiastically shared by young women or their mothers, and that women have long conspired to avoid the distasteful plans of their male kin and to promote matches that are desirable to the brides. Modern young village women, who have been educated in schools with Australian curricula and who have been exposed to non-indigenous patterns of courtship, insist on the right to choose their own mates. Conflict between these women and their kin is one important source of suicide in Kaliai.

Finally, an abused, powerless person may respond to mistreatment by extreme passivity or by committing suicide. In folk tales, a misused woman will allow herself to be publicly humiliated so that her kin are moved by pity or shame to come to her aid. She may cover herself with ashes, refuse to eat, and permit her tormentors to kick and burn her and take her personal possessions until her kin are shamed into defending her. If an abused person's relatives are insensitive and do not come to her assistance, then she is likely to kill herself. These alternatives are open to both men and women, and in oral literature both sexes respond to abuse with passivity or suicide. However, in real life the only male suicides for which I have data killed themselves either because they were unable to control their households of multiple wives or because they were shamed by their affines. It is notable that villagers consider these men to have been the victims of sorcery and, therefore, not acting of their own will.

THE CONTEXT OF SUICIDE

Although it is not restricted to women, suicide is becoming increasingly common in Kaliai and, in recent years has been restricted to women of reproductive age. I concentrate here on the suicide of women as a form of political strategy because Lusi women are ordinarily subject to male authority and are, therefore, usually less powerful than men of the same age. There are a number of cultural factors impinging on female status that are relevant to this discussion of suicide and that provide a context for understanding why a woman might choose self-destruction. First, a Lusi-Kaliai woman usually derives her social position from her association with a male, especially from her father or her husband. When she is a girl, the patriarchal ideal is that her sexuality is controlled by her father. According to this ideal, rights over her are transferred to her husband at marriage, for when a woman marries she becomes associated with her husband and his kin.

There is no avenue by which a woman can make a reputation for herself in the social-political system. There are no female leaders, nor is there a female term that is equivalent to the Lusi *maroni*, "male leader" or "bigman," and although the contributions of women to the system of ceremonial exchange are critical to it, women do not make names for themselves by their participation. The best that a Lusi-Kaliai woman can hope for in terms of personal renown is that her assistance will enable her husband to achieve fame as a *maroni*, for if he does she will also be honored and known as the "mother" or "female bone [support] of the village."

Lusi-Kaliai give ambiguous responses when they are asked about women's property rights. On the one hand, women say that the money that they earn from the sale of copra or from their wage labor belongs to them. On the other hand, married women say that they use the cash they earn to purchase things for their household and children or that they pool their resources with their husbands for the family welfare or to help the men achieve renown. People say that a woman may inherit from her parents, but they also claim that rights to the property that a woman inherits, and rights to the product of her labor, are transferred to her husband. Fathers cite this transferral of rights as the reason why they are reluctant to spend resources on their daughters if they have sons, and people may refer to it in a dispute over an inherited estate. David Counts and I discuss in detail a case in which a woman who attempted to exercise rights over her inherited property was informed by her kinsmen, who disputed her claim, that she had no right to inherit. They argued that because she was a married woman her property came under the control of her husband and would therefore, if she had inheritance rights, be lost to her kin group (Counts and Counts, 1974).

The limitations on female political and economic equality are highlighted by the norms of behavior that are explicitly expressed in public statements and in mythology. These norms declare that fathers and husbands are dominant and the masters of wives and children. Taken at face value, they assert that a Lusi-Kaliai woman should submit to her husband and to all her male kinsmen. The explicit ideal of male dominance, together with the fact that a Lusi-Kaliai woman's social position is derived from her relationship to a man, limits her ability to challenge male authority in the public forum. As a rule, women who publicly defy their menfolk are loudly condemned and risk violent retaliation. The inequity of physical strength between men and women makes overt defiance or acts of physical retaliation risky, but there are some Lusi-Kaliai women who are aggressive, assertive, and powerful. All of these women for whom I have data were first-born children and are the wives and/or daughters of powerful men.

While women do not usually respond to physical abuse, shame, or difficult and tense situations by committing suicide, there are some situations that create such profound shame that a woman's alternatives are limited or ineffective. It is under these circumstances that women commit suicide. The relationships created by marriage, particularly those between co-wives and between a woman and her affines, may be especially tense and conducive to intense humiliation. Polygyny and the resulting co-wife relations are especially fraught with tension and conflict; if the conflict cannot be contained, the result may be suicide, either by one of the wives (see the appendix to this chapter for the cases of Ruth and June) or by the husband (see the cases of Tomas, Nathan and Bill).

Obviously both women and men have affines, but the relationship is more likely to be difficult for a woman than for a man because married couples usually settle virilocally. As a result, a woman is in daily contact with her in-laws and is more vulnerable to the stresses inherent in affinal relationships characterized by cross-sex avoidance. The burden of responsibility for correct avoidance behavior is placed on the younger partner to the relationship or on the outsider who has married into the community. A woman who is alone with, eats in front of, talks to, or calls the name of her husband's father or brother is shamed, and any suggestion of sexual contact between them is intensely humiliating. I will elaborate on this point in my discussion of Sharon's suicide. It is sufficient to note here that the rule of in-law avoidance together with the potential for tension and shame in affinal relations limits the alternatives that are available to someone who has been humiliated by an in-law. If one is shamed by one's mother-in-law, for example, one cannot remove the shame or turn it back onto the perpetrator by taking the matter to court, by violence, or even by appealing to one's own relatives. In this case, if the humiliation is extreme and the shame is intolerable, the only appropriate and effective response may be suicide. The behavior of affines, spouses, or co-wives motivated ten of the twelve suicides or suicide attempts summarized in the appendix to this chapter.

When Lusi-Kaliai kill themselves it is customarily done by hanging or by drinking poison. Traditionally they drank a concoction, made of the *derris* (sp.) vine called *tuva* or *karavat* in Lusi, a concoction that is ordinarily used as a fish poison. Today people may also drink household bleach, mix an infusion of water with chemicals from flashlight batteries, or take a massive overdose of chloroquine phosphate, a malarial preventative. When Lusi-Kaliai speak of suicide they describe the method by which it occurred ("He hanged himself." "She drank poison."), they say *"ipamateai"* 'he killed himself', or they attribute responsibility for the death; *"tipamateai ngani posanga"* "they killed her with talk."

CASE STUDY 1: THE DEATH OF AGNES[2]

The events that lead to Agnes's death by hanging in 1975 began several months before when Victor returned to his home village, bringing with him a young woman from the Cape Gloucester area whom he wished to marry. His mother, Gloria, was furious and insisted that she would never accept a foreign bride and that Victor must take a local wife. Gloria then approached Agnes, who was aged sixteen, and encouraged her to seduce Victor, telling the girl that they would pay bridewealth for her if she could drive away the foreign woman and become

Victor's wife. Agnes agreed, for she had hoped to marry Victor, and one evening during an all-night ceremony the two of them slipped away together. Shortly thereafter the Gloucester woman returned to her home.

Although Agnes and Victor began to live openly as a married couple, no one had consulted her kinsmen about the arrangement and her paternal relatives were angry. They were embarrassed by Agnes's part in the shabby treatment of the modest, hard-working young woman that Victor had originally chosen; they resented Gloria's having approached Agnes in secret rather than entering into open negotiations with her relatives and making an initial bridewealth payment, as was proper; and they were furious with Agnes for compromising herself with Victor rather than confiding in her parents and taking their advice. To demonstrate their annoyance, they demanded that Victor's parents pay a bridewealth of 300 fathoms of shell money. This was not an unreasonable amount by local standards, but it was far above the official bridewealth maximum of 50 fathoms set by the local government council, an amount that Victor's parents had apparently expected to pay, and it was *demanded* rather than negotiated. Victor's parents announced that they would not pay the bridewealth and demanded that Agnes—whom they now charged with being promiscuous—leave their house where she and Victor had been living. They then began marriage negotiations with Karl for his daughter Rose, who was Agnes's patrilateral cross-cousin. Finally Victor and his parents returned to Cape Gloucester and, a few weeks later, Karl received a letter from Victor's parents formally asking that Rose marry Victor and Agnes received a letter from Victor, telling her that he would not marry her.

During the weeks after Victor returned to Cape Gloucester, Agnes's behavior changed. She cried frequently, she did not share a cooking fire with other women because they pointed her out to their children as an example of someone who did not behave properly, and two days before her death she began scratching messages on young coconuts—messages such as: "Goodby! I'll soon be leaving you": "I am an outlaw"; "I'm sorry I'll soon be leaving my people." A villager found some of these coconuts and took them to the house of Agnes's parents, but they were out. By evening the coconuts had been lost by young children, playing with them and the man had forgotten about them. The evening before her death, Agnes joined a group of women and directed the conversation to the subject of suicide, asking for details of other deaths, inquiring how the hanging knots were tied, and asking what happened after the death. The next morning, Agnes wrote a letter to her friend, Martha, who was also having marital problems. The letter asked Martha to tell Victor of her death and ended, "I'm going now. Later you follow me," a clear invitation for Martha to join her in death. Agnes asked a young kinsman of Martha's to deliver the letter to Martha, then she dressed in her finest clothing and slipped out of the village alone. A short while later she was found hanging by her neck from a tree beside one of the main paths to the nearby gardens.

In the afternoon, Agnes's parents returned to the village. Her mother went directly to the house where Agnes's body was lying and began to weep and caress her. The father staggered into the village plaza, fell writhing in the dirt and crying out, "Why did you kill my child? Why did you not kill me instead? Why did you kill my child?" Word of Agnes's death quickly spread along the coast, and the manager of the nearby plantation sent a telegram to the patrol officer at Cape Gloucester, asking him to come and investigate it. The following day, just as her family was preparing for Agnes's burial, the patrol officer arrived with Victor, his parents, and some obviously nervous policemen—one of whom asked me if I thought there would be a murder as soon as they left. The patrol officer held an inquest into the death and found that it was obviously a suicide and, therefore, not a matter for the government to deal with. He told the assembled villagers to settle the matter in a customary fashion but advised them that if there were bloodshed he would return and jail everyone involved.

Following the burial of Agnes, the villagers held a meeting to discuss responsibility for her death. One group of her relatives stated that no indemnity should be paid as there was no amount that could cancel out the wrong that had been done to the girl or bring her back to life. My consultants interpreted this as a statement of intent to kill Victor and his parents, probably by sorcery. Others reminded Agnes's kin that the patrol officer had ordered the community to settle the matter, using means that did not involve bloodshed and recommended that Victor's parents pay compensation to her maternal kin. Before the amount could be set, the villagers performed a ritual in which they interviewed Agnes's ghost to determine whether she had committed suicide because she was the victim of sorcery or whether she had done it of her own free will. The ritual ascertained that sorcery was not involved; had there been, then the sorcerer as well as Victor and his parents would have been culpable. Once this was determined, a group of disinterested elders met with both sets of parents and established a compensation payment. In January, 1976, four months after Agnes's death, Victor's parents paid 65 fathoms

of shell currency, 6 kina[3], and a pig. At the insistence of Victor's grandmother's brother, the payment was set above that recommended by the
elders because, as he told me, although no payment could erase his
"child's" wrong, it would perhaps emphasize true regret and help prevent
the retaliatory murder of Victor.

I have argued (Counts 1980) that Agnes's suicide was a political act
that enabled her to communicate, in a way that could not be ignored,
the message that she was a powerless figure, unjustly treated and caught
in a set of social relationships that she found intolerable but that she
could not change. She could reasonably expect that her suicide would
have certain consequences if she followed the culturally patterned rules
that govern the procedure that a person killing herself should follow.
Briefly these rules are as follows:

(1) She should not kill herself impulsively or in secret.
(2) She should warn others of her intention, using one of a number
    of recognized signals.
(3) She should dress in her finest clothing or in traditional costume
    before killing herself.
(4) She should kill herself in the presence of others or where her
    body would be discovered soon after her death.
(5) She should leave a final message that informed her survivors of
    the identity of the person who was responsible for the circum-
    stances leading to her death.

Agnes's death met these criteria. All the villagers with whom I
talked agreed that by singling out Victor to be notified of her death,
she had accused him of being responsible for it. She knew that in spite
of the fact that her death was self-inflicted, her fellows would consider
her suicide to be the result of a form of homicide. The phrase, "They
kill her with talk," and her father's cry, "Why did you kill my child?" express this assumption of culpability. She knew that her kin would demand compensation for her death, and that they might take revenge.
Victor and his parents would bear the disgrace of knowing they had
caused her death, the financial cost of compensation to her kin, and the
fear that they might be killed as well. Finally, her death would remove
her shame. Everyone — her relatives who had failed to support her, her
neighbors who had slandered her and gossiped about her, and Victor
and his kin who had wronged her — would realize how deeply she had
been shamed and would feel sorrow for her and regret their treatment
of her.

Agnes's behavior is consistent with Epstein's analysis of the discharge of shame (1984:42-43). He argues that the mode of discharging shame in Papua, New Guinea involves a balance of inward- and outward-directed action that combines "aggression against the self with its re-direction to another" (ibid.:43). One may accomplish this by destroying his own property, by self-injury, or by the ultimate combination of these two acts: by suicide.

Given the fact that the person killing herself communicates to her survivors a message about the cause of her misery, hoping thereby to direct the reaction of her kin and friends, suicide may be described as a political act. But what of the suicide that does not communicate an un-ambiguous message? What of the self-killing that does not follow the rules? How may such an act be explained by the survivors, and how does the community respond?

CASE STUDY 2: THE DEATH OF SHARON

In 1979, Sharon, a married woman with a number of young chil-dren, drank household bleach and died of self-administered poison. Al-though I was not present in the village at the time of her death, I discussed the event at length with many villagers in 1981. People agreed on a number of facts:

(1) Sharon had been involved in an affair with Stud, her husband's classificatory brother, an affair that resulted in her pregnancy. Because she behaved in an irresponsible manner, leaving her small children alone for long periods while she met Stud, many of my consultants sus-pected that he had enchanted her with love magic.

(2) Sharon's husband, Paul, was aware of the affair. On several occa-sions they quarreled violently and he beat her. The possibility that she had been seduced by love magic did not absolve her of responsibility for her behavior.

(3) On the night following the 1979 Independence Day celebrations, Sharon did not return home. Her husband, and all of the people with whom I discussed the case, assumed that she spent the night with Stud. Paul met her upon her return home and they quarreled violently.

(4) Late on the afternoon of her return, Sharon went alone to the seep spring where women wash clothing. Shortly thereafter, Puri heard Sharon calling, "Come, I'm dying!" Puri ran to the spring and saw Sharon drink the last of a bottle of household bleach. She tried

unsuccessfully to induce vomiting and then she ran for help. By the time her fellow villagers had carried Sharon home she was comatose. She died that night despite intensive efforts to resuscitate her.

(5) Paul and Stud both paid compensation to Sharon's parents for her death, but no payment was made by Stud to Paul. Payment of compensation between brothers, even classificatory ones, is inappropriate among the Lusi-Kaliai because brothers share rights in land and in resources.

(6) The relatives of Paul and Stud were shamed by the publicity resulting from the suicide, and four households—headed by one of their senior kinsmen and including Paul's full brother—moved out of the village and built a small hamlet located about thirty minutes by canoe down the coast. Paul, a school catechist, moved to a small house on the school grounds. Sharon's parents took custody of her and Paul's children.

Although people agreed on these facts, there was no consensus about the meaning of Sharon's death, for she had not followed the rules of procedure for suicide. As a result, the message sent by her death was ambiguous, and people were uncomfortable discussing the circumstances surrounding it and were in disagreement about the assignment of culpability and/or responsibility for it. Some argued that Paul's payment of compensation to Sharon's parents demonstrated that he was responsible, with one woman commenting that Sharon, being caught between love magic and a violent husband, might have thought she had no choice. If a woman is beaten too severely, she added, she may think suicide is her only recourse. One of Sharon's relatives opined that Paul had been seen by children, forcing Sharon to drink the poison. Thus he had actually murdered her. Others argued that Sharon was responsible: she was shamed by her pregnancy and was killed by her self-induced shame. Sharon had behaved selfishly and irresponsibly by killing herself, in one woman's opinion. "Sharon was thinking only of herself, not of her children," she said. "Who will raise her babies now?" Still others argued that nobody was responsible. Suicide is common in some families, one man observed, and Sharon was reacting to shame in the same way as had her kin before her. The possibility that Sharon had been ensorceled was ruled out by a divination ritual similar to the one performed after the death of Agnes.

In a discussion elsewhere of the events leading up to Sharon's death, David Counts and I argue that the adultery between Sharon and Stud was different from common adultery because they were affines (Counts and Counts 1984). The Lusi-Kaliai consider affinal adultery to be animal-like behavior: people who engage in it are said to be "acting like dogs." The seriousness with which they view this behavior is signaled by the fact that people never joke or gossip about it lightly, and by the fact that in real life and in oral narratives people who even suspect that others believe they are involved in a relationship of this type may kill themselves (see the case of Biliku in the appendix to this chapter). The Lusi-Kaliai behave toward affinal adultery in somewhat the same way that the Arapesh respond to the consumption of human flesh. Tuzin reports that his Arapesh informants insisted that Japanese cannibalism during World War II could only be explained as "a fear inspired act of deculturated madness" (Tuzin 1983:70). By denying that the Japanese ate human flesh simply because they were hungry, Tuzin argues, the Arapesh were able to maintain that cannibalism is an unthinkable act, an act that is not an option for normal people even in a crisis. By the same token, the Lusi-Kaliai consider affinal adultery to be an act inappropriate for normal humans; they deny that it occurs and respond to suggestions of it with disgust and horror; and they have no legal mechanisms in place that adequately deal with the problems that are raised when such behavior does occur.

The affair between Sharon and Stud was, then, an unspeakable relationship and, as far as I am able to ascertain, although it was no secret in the village it was never brought into the public domain. With Sharon's pregnancy, however, the matter could no longer be kept within the confines of the kin group for, according to traditional Lusi-Kaliai conception theory, the appearance of the child would publicly proclaim its paternity and would be a constant reminder to everyone of the shameful behavior of Sharon and Stud.[4]

When I returned to Kaliai in 1985 I learned that the ambiguous nature of Sharon's death had, in the view of her co-villagers, resulted in fatal consequences for Paul. Sharon's father, convinced that Paul had caused Sharon's death, had engaged the services of a sorcerer to kill him. Following his death, Paul's kin held a village meeting at which the sorcerer admitted that he had ensorceled Paul and stated that he had been hired to do it by Sharon's father.[5] The sorcerer then fled the area and was severely beaten by the relatives of a subsequent victim.

Sharon's suicide was different from Agnes's in that she did not follow the rules that would permit her to attain the culturally recognized end of assigning culpability for her act while at the same time removing her shame. Instead the consequences of her act were (a) the public recognition of her adulterous affair—behavior that her fellows considered to be appropriate for dogs, not humans; (b) ambivalence and confusion on the part of other villagers; (c) the shaming of her husband's kin, including persons who had no part in the affair, and the fissioning of their kin group; and (d) the death by sorcery of her husband.

Perhaps the most important factor in the suicide, for the purposes of this discussion, was that Sharon was not a blameless and powerless victim who was responding to the abusive and/or shaming behavior of others. Nonetheless, her kin attributed culpability (although she had left no message that legitimately enabled them to do this) and took revenge as though her suicide had been carried out in accordance with the rules.

CASE STUDY 3: THE DEATH OF GALIKI

Let us now consider the public reaction to the suicide of a woman whose behavior was considered by her neighbors to be blameless but whose death did not follow the rules and was, therefore, ambiguous and open to interpretation.

Galiki, a woman from a distant village, married the son of an important man and bore him several children. Her husband was absent from the village for long periods of time, and although other women insisted that her behavior was irreproachable, her husband, Akono, came to believe that she was conducting an affair during his absence. The weekend before her death the two fought constantly. On Monday, after a trip to the gardens to gather food, she was sitting in her cook house preparing sweet potatoes for her children's supper when she suddenly burst out of the house crying, "Come, help me! I'm dying!" staggered into center of her household compound, and became unconscious. People attempted to force her to drink sweetened milk and tossed her in a pig net, hoping to cause her to vomit the poison she was believed to have taken, but she never regained consciousness and was soon dead. The nurse from the Kaliai Health Centre came to examine Galiki's body and listed her death as suicide. These events occurred about a month before my return to Kaliai in 1985. All my consultants agree on the above outline of facts. Other circumstances surrounding Galiki's death are controversial and a matter of interpretation. The various versions, which I summarize below, disagree on the facts, emphasize some events, and ignore or discount others, and either accept or challenge eyewitness accounts of Galiki's last conscious moments. Some of the interpretations accept the death as a suicide while others suggest direct homicide. All seem to have been based, at least in part, on the interpreter's relationship to Akono, for Galiki had no family living nearby. No divination to ascertain the possibility of sorcery was done for Galiki: she had no resident close kin to perform it. The various interpretations of Galiki's death were as follows:

(1) Akono's close relatives and affines, including witnesses to Galiki's last words, either did not comment on the relationship between Galiki and Akono or emphasized that the dissension between the two was mutual and that neither party was blameless. They interpreted Galiki's death as a suicide and stressed that her dying words were that she had consumed fish poison or household bleach mixed with fish poison, and they emphasized that she had made statements at least a day earlier, indicating that she was planning to kill herself. They attributed no culpability for her death but rather suggested that it demonstrated the instability and unpredictability of women. As one man commented to me, "I don't understand women. Three of them have drunk poison in less than three weeks. If anyone says the slightest cross word to a woman or if there is even a trivial disagreement, she may kill herself. Men don't behave in this way. Only women."

(2) Persons distantly related to Akono agreed that Galiki had taken poison, but they disagreed as to whether she had drunk fish poison, bleach, an overdose of chloroquine phosphate tablets, or some mixture of the above. Some people, notably women, emphasized the brutality of the abuse Galiki suffered from Akono before her death and stressed the pity and distress they felt at her mistreatment. Because they were not related to her, they said, they had no right to interfere, and those who attempted to were threatened or shamed by Akono. One woman commented that she and other women had gone to mourn Galiki only briefly because they were offended by Akono's display of grief: " 'Why are you crying?' we asked ourselves. 'You killed her!' "

This same woman also related that shortly after Galiki's death her ghost was seen in another village, asking for paper so that she could write a letter to Akono and his new wife. When I asked if Akono were intending to marry again, my informant responded that *she* did not know (implying that Galiki's ghost would know), and added that Akono must be planning to remarry or he would not have abused Galiki so. It is notable that some people attributed to Galiki's ghost the behavior that would have made her suicide unambiguous and would have established culpability for it.

(3) Persons unrelated to Akono by other than distant and indirect affinal ties disagreed with the interpretation of suicide. They noted that neither the odour of bleach nor fish poison (both strong and unmistakable smells) were on Galiki's breath at the time of her death. They also recounted that as she was tossed in the pig net, Galiki bled profusely from her nose and mouth and observed that her skin was black from head to toe. Also, they reported, when the women dressed her body for burial, they found that it was covered with welts, open cuts, and bruises. They argued that these physical manifestations were inconsistent with the effects of death by poison that they had previously witnessed. Rather, they concluded, Galiki's condition was that of a person who had been beaten until she suffered fatal injuries. They claimed that no one but Akono's close relatives had actually heard Galiki say that she had drunk poison; other witnesses had said that she was unable to speak following her initial cry that she was dying, and that she could only point to her abdomen before losing consciousness. They suspected that Akono's kin conspired to say that Galiki died from drinking poison in order to protect him from legal prosecution. One man commented that traditional wisdom taught that a killer's appearance changed: his eyes became hollow, his cheeks became sunken, his skin lost its lustre, and he became emaciated. This, he observed, aptly described Akono.

DISCUSSION

Galiki's and Sharon's suicides illustrate the variety of responses that people may have to an ambiguous suicide. Galiki's death did not follow the cultural rules for suicide. She did not prepare for her death by destroying her property and dressing in her finery, but instead she was engaged in an ordinary household task when, apparently, she suddenly quit her work and drank poison.[6] Also, she left no clear message assigning culpability for her death. The aspects of her behavior that are consistent with a culturally patterned suicide—her (ignored) statement of intent the day before her death, her words that she had consumed poison, and the appearance of her ghost to give a message to Akono thereby pointing to his guilt—were not widely witnessed and are controversial. When a death such as Galiki's does not follow the commonly known cultural pattern for suicide, the message of the death is ambiguous and people may interpret it in a variety of ways. There are a number of factors that may influence this interpretation.

First, people judge the behavior of the suicide before her death. They may determine that she was guilty of acts that might explain the slander and/or abuse that led to her death and question whether her suicide was an attempt to escape from the consequences of shameful behavior. These factors were significant in the community's response to Sharon's death. Or, they may conclude that the suicide's behavior was blameless and that she is the innocent victim of abuse. This was the judgment in Agnes's case and, for all but Akono's close kin, in Galiki's.

Second, they attempt to determine the nature of the death. Was it the result of sorcery causing deep depression and thereby leading to suicide? Was the death by the person's own hand or by the hand of others? Ritual steps may be taken to rule out sorcery, regardless of whether the suicide is ambiguous or unambiguous, as was the case in the deaths of both Agnes and Sharon. If a divination ritual points to the presence of sorcery, then the sorcerer is also considered to be culpable. His guilt does not, however, excuse the actions of those others whose mistreatment of the victim precipitated her suicide.

Third, in Kaliai the death of a person in the prime of life always involves culpability, even if the victim's behavior is considered to be censurable. In the case of an ambiguous suicide, the events surrounding the death may be interpreted to lessen the ambiguity and to allow the assignment of culpability. This was the end achieved by the message given by Galiki's ghost.

Fourth, in the traditional legal system, death by one's own hand and death at the hand of others are both regarded as forms of homicide, and the responses of the community are similar. Papua, New Guinea law prohibits physical retribution or personal vengeance for homicide, so the relatives of the victim may exact compensatory payments and/or engage the services of a sorcerer. Payment may, but does not necessarily, preclude vengeance by sorcery—as the case of Sharon illustrates.

Fifth, people are well aware that the legal system of Papua, New Guinea distinguishes between suicide and homicide. Culpability for suicide is not a felony; culpability for homicide is. Their evaluation of which system should be applied in a particular case is a factor in the interpretation that people give of the circumstances surrounding a death. Controversy surrounding a death that is defined as suicide may be settled by traditional means, whereas homicide necessarily involves the police and the courts. Culpable people and their close kin always seem to prefer that disputes be settled at the lowest possible level—by customary procedure rather than by government law; by village officials rather than by provincial or national authorities. In Galiki's case, Akono accepted culpability for her suicide and made reparation payments to her kin. Government officials did not become involved.

APPENDIX: SUMMARY OF
CASE STUDIES OF SUICIDES[7]

RUTH attempted suicide after her husband had taken the side of her co-wife, had publicly shamed her, and had beaten her. She prepared fish poison and drank it in the presence of other villagers who forced her to vomit the poison. Her act influenced her husband's behavior, for although Ruth continued to fight with her co-wife, her husband did not again publicly shame her and he refrained from beating her for at least a year.

JUNE was barren so, under pressure from his kin, her husband agreed to take a second wife. In response, June drank fish poison. Although she was forced to vomit and did not die, the matter of her husband's remarriage was dropped.

BILL fathered two children by Mary and after the birth of the second child he announced his plan to take her as his second wife. His angry wife, shouting that she would kill him first, grabbed an axe and chased Bill out of the village. Weeping with shame, Bill was found in the forest, preparing to drink fish poison. His relatives persuaded him to return to the village and to end all discussion of a possible marriage with Mary.

NANCY drank fish poison after being publicly accused by her affines of having an affair while her husband was working at a nearby plantation. She died and her husband paid compensation to her relatives.

BILIKU'S elderly, senile father-in-law exposed his genitals to her while they were alone in her house. She was shamed by his act and suspected her husband and others of gossiping about her and ridiculing her. After accusing her husband of shaming her, she broke her canoe with an axe, prepared fish poison, and drank the concoction in the presence of others. She died, and her husband and his kin paid compensation to her relatives.

TOMAS beat one of his wives for fighting with the other. The male relatives of the beaten wife publicly shamed Tomas and berated him for the beating. Tomas distributed pigs to them and then drank fish poison in the presence of his wife and children. The abused wife's kin were held culpable for Tomas's suicide and they paid compensation to his kin.

NATHAN, a close kinsman of Tomas, was shamed by his inability to contain the fighting of his two wives. He prepared fish poison, climbed to the top of a tree, placed a rope around his neck, called out his intentions, drank the poison, and jumped. The deaths of Tomas and Nathan both occurred in the early 1900s and my consultants attribute their suicides to sorcery. Agnes, Sharon and Elaine, whose death is described below, were descendants of Nathan and Tomas.

ELAINE, the teen-aged daughter of Sharon and Paul, was called home from the town where she was living with a kinswoman, Beth, to attend the funeral of her father. When she wished to return to town, her grandparents refused to allow her to go. She sneaked away, returned to town, and resumed her affair with a man that Beth considered to be of bad character and an unsuitable husband. After Beth scolded her, Elaine went into her room and drank bleach. Beth's parents paid compensation for Elaine's death to her Elaine's closer relatives. Some villagers speculate that Agnes, Elaine and Sharon may be the victims of the inherited residue of the sorcery that was used to kill Tomas and Nathan.

BELINDA was at the area sports field playing competitive basketball. On the way home her husband berated her for flirting with men and beat her. She prepared a concoction of battery acid and water and drank it. Her husband paid compensation to her parents for her death.

BARBARA drank fish poison after having been beaten by her husband. No further details are available about her death.

ETHEL hanged herself, allegedly after having been beaten by Oscar, her husband. Both were originally from the New Guinea Highlands and had been resident in West New Britain for less than a year. Oscar accompanied Ethel's body home and, according to a news broadcast, was held in protective custody until his family paid a large compensation to Ethel's relatives. In spite of the payment, Oscar's wife's kin met the airplane returning him home and murdered him with axes.

CATHERINE wished to marry a young man of whom her parents disapproved. After a tearful confrontation she climbed to the top of a coconut tree and drank fish poison. Although people realized that she was missing, her decomposed body was not found for several days.

NOTES

1. Research on which this paper is based was conducted in West New Britain Province, Papua, New Guinea, in 1966-67 with the support of the National Science

Foundation and Southern Illinois University; in 1971 with the support of the University of Waterloo and the Wenner-Gren Foundation; in 1975-76 with the support of the Canada Council and the University of Waterloo; and in 1981 and 1985 with the support of the Social Sciences and Humanities Research Council of Canada and the University of Waterloo.

2. This case study is discussed in detail in Counts (1980, 1984). All names have been changed in the case studies to protect individual privacy.

3. The kina is the Papua, New Guinea unit of currency. In 1976 it was at par with the Australian dollar.

4. The traditional Lusi-Kaliai view is that fetuses are composed entirely of their father's semen and are built up by multiple acts of sexual intercourse. It is possible for a child to have two or more fathers. If there are no more than two, they can be identified by the time a child reaches puberty because, as it matures, a child increasingly exhibits paternal characteristics—particularly the carriage, the walk, and to a lesser degree the facial features of his father(s). If there are three or more men involved, the paternal substances are so mixed as to make positive identification impossible. See Counts and Counts (1983) for more details on Lusi-Kaliai ideas about conception, fetal development, and the relationship between a child and its genitors.

5. There has been no formal legal or medical relationship established between the actions of the sorcerer and the death of Paul. However, none of my consultants expressed any doubt that the sorcerer had done as he had claimed or that his actions had resulted in Paul's death.

6. Galiki was an outsider in her husband's village, being from a distant village and a different language group. It may be that her failure to follow the Kaliai rules of suicide was due to ignorance on her part. I do not know the rules of suicide of Galiki's society.

7. A more detailed discussion of these cases as well as details of suicides recounted in Kaliai oral literature is found in Counts (1984).

REFERENCES

Akin, D.: Suicide and women in East Kwaio, Malaita. In F. X. Hezel, D. H. Rubinstein, & G. M. White (Eds.) *Culture, youth and suicide in the Pacific.* Honolulu: Pacific Islands Studies Program, 1985, 198-220.

Berndt, R. M.: *Excess and restraint.* Chicago: University of Chicago Press, 1982.

Brown, M. F.: The dark side of progress. Paper presented at 44th International Congress of Americanists, Manchester, England, 1982.

Counts, D. A.: Fighting back is not the way. *American Ethnologist,* 7: 332-351, 1980.

Counts, D. A.: Revenge suicide by Lusi women. In D. O'Brien & S. Tiffany (Eds.) *Rethinking women's roles.* Berkeley: University of California Press, 1984, 71-93.

Counts, D. A.: Female suicide and wife abuse. *Suicide & Life-Threatening Behavior,* 17: 194-204, 1987.

Counts, D. A., & Counts, D. R.: Father's water equals mother's milk. *Mankind,* 14: 46-56, 1983.

Counts, D. A., & Counts, D. R.: People who act like dogs. Paper presented at conference on Deviance in a Cross-Cultural Context, Waterloo, Ontario, 1984.

Epstein, A. L.: *The experience of shame in Melanesia.* London: Royal Anthropological Institute, 1984.

Frankel, S.: *The Huli response to illness.* Cambridge: Cambridge University Press, 1986.

Gegeo, D. W., & Watson-Gegeo, K. A.: Patterns of suicide in West Kwara'ae, Solomon Islands. In F. X. Hezel, D. H. Rubinstein, & G. W. White (Eds.) *Culture, youth and suicide in the Pacific.* Honolulu: Pacific Islands Studies Program, 1985, 182-197.

Giddens, A.: Suicide, attempted suicide and the suicidal threat. *Man,* 64: 115-116, 1964.

Healey, C.: Women and suicide in New Guinea. *Social Analysis,* 2: 89-106, 1979.

Hoskin, J. O., Friedman, M. I., & Cawte, J. E.: A high incidence of suicide in a preliterate society. *Psychiatry,* 32: 200-210, 1969.

Jeffreys, M. D. W.: Samsonic suicide or suicide of revenge among Africans. *African Studies,* 19: 118-122, 1952.

Johnson, P. L.: When dying is better than living. *Ethnology,* 20: 325-334, 1981.

Marshall, M.: *Weekend warriors.* Palo Alto: Mayfield, 1979.

McKellin, W. H.: The meanings of Managalese suicide. Paper delivered at the Annual Meeting of the ASAO, Salem, Massachusetts, 1985.

Panoff, M.: Suicide and social control in New Britain. *Bijdrogen: Tot de Taal-Land-en Volkenkunde,* 133: 44-62, 1977.

Poole, F. J. P.: Among the boughs of the hanging tree. In F. X. Hezel, D. H. Rubinstein & G. W. White (Eds.) *Culture, youth and suicide in the Pacific.* Honolulu: Pacific Islands Studies Program, 1985, 152-181.

Reay, M.: *The Kuma.* Melbourne: Melbourne University Press, 1959.

Sivers, H.: Broken hearts and pots. Paper presented at the 44th International Congress of Americanists, Manchester, England, 1982.

Strathern, A.: Why is shame on the skin? *Ethnology,* 14: 347-356, 1975.

Strathern, M.: *Women in between.* London: Seminar Press, 1972.

Tuzin, D.: Cannibalism and Arapesh cosmology. In P. Brown & D. Tuzin (Eds.) *The ethnography of cannibalism.* New York: Society for Psychological Anthropology, 1983, 61-71.

CHAPTER 9

SUICIDE AND THE MENSTRUAL CYCLE

DAVID LESTER

A GOOD DEAL of research has explored the relationship between the incidence of suicidal behavior and the phase of the menstrual cycle. We will review the research in this chapter and explore its implications for our understanding of the differences in suicidal behavior.

Attempted Suicide

Dalton (1959) investigated female attempted suicides and noted a peak in the attempted suicide rate during the bleeding phase, with subsidiary peaks during the premenstrual and ovulation phases.[1] Mandell and Mandell (1967) studied callers to a suicide prevention center and found an excess of females in the premenstrual and bleeding phases. Wetzel, et al. (1969) also studied callers to a suicide prevention center and found the women to be menstruating more often than one would expect by chance, but no increase in the likelihood of women calling during the premenstrual phase. Trautman (1961) also reported an excess of attempted suicide during the bleeding phase of the cycle.

Tonks, et al. (1968) examined female attempted suicides and found peaks around the bleeding phase and the ovulation phase. (Tonks's results were not statistically significant. Furthermore, he noted the number of days prior to the next period, and he used 28 days as the length of the cycle for all women, even for those with cycles longer than 28 days.

---

1. Dalton also found a greater frequency of general psychiatric admissions, depression and schizophrenic attacks during this phase.

This increased the number of patients supposedly attempting suicide 28 days before a period.) Glass, et al. (1971) studied female psychiatric emergencies and found that the premenstrual females were more likely to have suicidal ideation.

On the other hand, Buckle, et al. (1965) reported no variation in attempted suicide over the menstrual cycle, either for the younger or for the older females in the sample. Birtchnell and Floyd (1974, 1975) found no association between attempted suicide and the menstrual cycle in a sample of emergency room patients. Holding and Minkoff (1973) found no association between attempts at suicide and the phase of the menstrual cycle (even when age, pregnancy, suicidal intent, marital status and premenstrual symptom scores were controlled). Pallis and Holding (1976) also found no variation in attempted suicide over the menstrual cycle. Ekberg, et al. (1986) found no association between the incidence of self-poisoning and the menstrual cycle, either for suicidal or nonintentional overdoses or for any of the particular toxic agents ingested.

Dalton noted that those women attempting suicide during the premenstrual and bleeding phases of the cycle were younger than the others. Tonks, et al. found that age, parity, and premenstrual symptoms had no effect on the association. However, those women living with a man attempted suicide sooner after the first day of the menstrual cycle than those living alone. Tonks, et al. also looked at the association in different subgroups of the sample. They found that, for parous females with premenstrual symptoms, suicide attempts were less likely premenstrually (as opposed to postmenstrually) than for parous females without premenstrual symptoms.

Wetzel, et al., who studied callers to a suicide prevention center, found that women who were in the luteal phase or the bleeding phase of the cycle had the highest self-judged seriousness of suicidal intent. This was especially so if they had a history of suicide attempts. These women also more often reported having a family member who was depressed or suicidal. The callers to the center did not differ from women who had never sought psychiatric help in the incidence of dysmenorrhea.

Pallis and Holding compared premenstrual suicide attempters with the other attempters and found no differences in age, marital status, depression or premenstrual symptom scores, but they did have higher suicidal intent. Birtchnell and Floyd compared attempted suicides and normal controls and found no differences in premenstrual disturbances, the number of days of bleeding or the number using birth control pills.

The attempted suicides were more likely to have a regular cycle of 28 days, to be late for their next period, and to be pregnant. (They were also younger and more likely to be unmarried.)

Finlay (1970) found no differences in the incidence of dysmenorrhea in suicidal and nonsuicidal college students. Wetzel, et al. (1971a, 1971b) studied callers to a suicide prevention center. Compared to normal controls, the callers reported more premenstrual symptoms and more interference in their lives from the symptoms. Callers during the bleeding phase reported more serious suicidal behavior. Self-ratings of suicidal risk were higher for those in the bleeding and luteal phases. Rosenthal, et al. (1972) found that wrist cutters were more likely to have irregular menses and to feel negative toward menstruation than females using other methods for attempting suicide.

These results are not easy to summarize.

(1) First, it appears that the research is inconsistent on the basic association. Five studies out of the ten find an excess of suicidal attempts or suicidal preoccupation during the bleeding phase, three find a premenstrual increase and two find a luteal/ovulation phase increase. Interestingly, no studies report a decrease during these phases. Thus, we may conclude that the association is present but weak.[2]

(2) The research also shows that a variety of other factors need to be taken into account, including parity, dysmenorrhea and amenorrhea, premenstrual symptoms, and days of bleeding as well as psychiatric and sociodemographic variables.

(3) The research also suggests the importance of measuring the serious of the suicidal intent as well as the actual occurrence of a suicide attempt.

Completed Suicides

Only two studies on completed studies have appeared. McKinnon, et al. (1959) carried out autopsies on women who had killed themselves and found that the suicide rate was greatest during the mid-luteal phase of the cycle (days 17-23). (The same distribution was found, however, for women who died from accidents and diseases.) Ribeiro (1962) studied a small sample of Hindu women who had immolated themselves and found that 19 of the 22 were menstruating (while two others were pregnant).

---

2. We must remember that we do not know whether there is an excess of suicide attempts during the premenstrual and bleeding phases or a deficit during other phases of the menstrual cycle.

Interestingly, Roland, et al. (1986) found higher levels of testerone (the male sex hormone) in the blood of male completed suicides than in men dying suddenly from other causes.

Explanations

During the bleeding phase of the menstrual cycle, the levels of circulating estrogen and progesterone are low (see, for example, Guyton, 1959), and during the mid-luteal phase the levels of circulating estrogen and progesterone are high. Perhaps the level of these hormones is important in the timing of suicide attempts?

This raises several interesting research questions. First, what is the suicide rate during pregnancy (when the estrogen level is low)? Rosenberg and Silver (1965) have reported that the rate of completed suicides in pregnant women is low. They estimated that the completed suicide rate of pregnant women was about one-sixth of the expected rate. Barno (1967) estimated the suicide rate in pregnant women to be 0.03 per 100,000 per year as compared to a rate of about six for women in general. Lewis and Fay (1981) looked at 2.3 million births and found only six ante-partum completed suicides and eleven post-partum, evidence for the rarity of suicide in pregnant women.

Whitlock and Edwards (1968) reviewed estimates of the incidence of pregnancy among completed suicides, and these ranged from 3 percent to 20 percent, with 5 percent appearing to be the most reasonable estimate. For attempted suicides, the incidence of pregnant women ranged from one percent to 12 percent, with six percent appearing to be a reasonable estimate. They examined a sample of females who had attempted suicide and compared those who were pregnant with those who were not. The pregnant females who had attempted suicide were younger than those who were not pregnant but did not differ in marital status, religion or social class. Only about 47 percent of the pregnancies were conceived in wedlock by the husband. Of the 30 cases, the pregnancy played a precipitating role in five cases, a partial role in eight cases, and no role in 17 cases.

Of interest is the fact that attempts at suicide were equally common during the first two trimesters of pregnancy but rare during the third trimester. Rayburn, et al. (1984) found a higher incidence of women who had taken drug overdoses calling a poison control center during the first trimester than during the second and third trimesters.

A second important question is the suicide rate of women on the pill. Lester (1969) suggested that the birth control pill could have an ameliorative effect on suicidal behavior in females, but had no evidence to support such a hypothesis. Birtchnell and Floyd (1974) found no differences in the use of the pill in samples of attempted suicides and normal controls. However, Kane, et al. (1966) have reported using Enovid to successfully treat a suicidal psychotic woman.

Recently, Vessey et al. (1985) found that the attempted suicide rate in women on the pill did not differ from the rate of those using an intrauterine device (though both of these groups had a higher rate than women using a diaphragm). The length of time on the pill was not related to the rate of attempted suicide.

Lester (1969a) also noted that the hormonal changes accompanying menopause might affect the incidence of suicide. Interestingly here, completed suicide rates for women do peak in middle age, and thereupon drop, while completed suicide rates in men continue to rise with age.

Winston (1969) noted that disturbance in the tryptophan metabolism along the kynurenine pathway were associated with mood changes (Dewhurst, 1968) and that these disturbances occur just prior to the onset of menstruation. He speculated that this may be the mechanism underlying the association between suicidal behavior and the phase of the menstrual cycle. However, this hypothesis requires evidence that the sex hormones affect the tryptophan metabolism.

In Chapter 10, Lester proposes a dopaminergic theory of suicide based upon a theory of depression put forward by Skutsch (1981) in which depression is caused by high levels of dopamine in the central nervous system. Skutsch hypothesized that estrogen suppresses dopamine release, leading to low levels of dopamine. Thus, when the level of circulating estrogen is low, depression and therefore suicide should be more likely, which is the case during the premenstrual and bleeding phases of the menstrual cycle.

Struve (1985) found that attempted suicide was more likely in females with paroxysmal EEGs who had been taking oral contraceptives. Thus, the levels of estrogen (or progesterone) may increase the risk of suicide in those with paroxysmal electical activity in the brain (Lester, 1987b).

Broverman, et al. (1968) noted that females are better at tasks that are based upon past experience and which are evaluated in terms of speed and accuracy, while males are better at tasks which require inhibition or delay of initial responses to obvious stimulus attributes in favor of responses to less obvious stimulus attributes. They argued that these (and other) differences in perceptual motor functioning were a result of differences in the adrenergic and cholinergic neural processes. Lester (1974) rephrased this idea in terms of differences in the sympathetic and parasympathetic divisions of the autonomic nervous system. These differences in the functioning of the autonomic nervous system may in turn be dependent upon the sex hormones.

Broverman, et al. argued that estrogens tend to increase the activity of the sympathetic division much more than androgens do. The sympathetic division has a mobilizing function and prepares the organism for action. (The parasympathetic division works toward protection, conservation and relaxation of the organism when action is not required.) Eysenck (1967) sees sympathetic activity as the basis for neuroticism, and thus we might argue that the level of circulating estrogens affects the degree of neuroticism. Since the level of circulating estrogen is highest during the luteal phase of the menstrual cycle, suicide might be more common during this phase.

Thus, we can see that estrogens may be implicated in dopaminergic pathways in the brain, paroxysmal EEGs and the sympathetic division of the autonomic nervous system. At a more general level, sex hormones have been implicated in aggressive behavior (Berkowitz, 1962), and Lester (1987a) has discussed the evidence that suicide can be seen as an aggressive behavior. Scott and Fredericson (1951) have suggested that the sex hormones may have an effect by changing the sensitivity of organism to painful stimuli and thus their response to these stimuli.

Of course, psychological explanations of the variation in suicidal behavior over the menstrual cycle can be proposed. However, the possibility remains strong that the sex hormones do exert a physiological influence on the suicidal behavior, though the mechanism by which they do so remains unclear.

One final caveat is warranted here. It is important to show that the sex hormones affect suicidal behavior in particular rather than psychological disturbance in general. It will be of less interest if estrogens, for example, raise the level of general psychological disturbance as is proposed in the Eysenck/Lester hypothesis discussed above rather than having a specific impact on suicidal behavior.

DISCUSSION

Although psychological explanations can be proposed for the sex difference in suicidal behavior, these explanations, if valid, do not eliminate the possibility that the sex hormones may have a direct physiological role to play in explaining the sex differences in suicidal behavior. We have seen in this chapter that possible physiological mechanism involving estrogens in particular are quite compatible with physiological theories of depression and suicide.

REFERENCES

Barno, A.: Criminal abortion deaths, illegitimate pregnancy deaths and suicides in pregnancy. *American Journal of Obstetrics and Gynecology,* 98: 356-367, 1967.

Berkowitz, L.: *Aggression.* New York: McGraw-Hill, 1962.

Birtchnell, J., & Floyd, S.: Attempted suicide and the menstrual cycle. *Journal of Psychosomatic Research,* 18: 361-369, 1974.

Birtchnell, J., & Floyd, S.: Further menstrual characteristics of suicide attempters. *Journal of Psychosomatic Research,* 19: 81-85, 1975.

Broverman, D. M., Klaiber, E. L., Kobayashi, Y., & Vogel, W.: Roles of activation and inhibition in sex differences in cognitive abilities. *Psychological Review,* 75: 23-50, 1968.

Buckle, R. C., Linane, J., & McConaghy, N.: Attempted suicides presenting at the Alfred Hospital, Melbourne. *Medical Journal of Australia,* 1: 754-758, 1965.

Dalton, K.: Menstruation and acute psychiatric illness. *British Medical Journal,* 1: 148-149, 1959.

Dewhurst, W. G.: New theory of cerebral amine function and its clinical application. *Nature,* 218: 1130-1133, 1968.

Ekberg, O., Jacobsen, D., Sorum, Y., & Aass, G.: Self-poisoning and the menstrual cycle. *Acta Psychiatrica Scandinavia,* 73: 239-241, 1986.

Eysenck, H. J.: *The biological basis of personality.* Springfield: Thomas, 1967.

Finlay, S.: Suicide and self-injury in Leeds University students. *Proceedings of the 5th International Congress on Suicide Prevention.* Vienna: LASP, 1970.

Glass, G., Heninger, G., Lansky, M., & Talan, K.: Psychiatric emergencies related to the menstrual cycle. *American Journal of Psychiatry,* 128: 705-711, 1971.

Guyton, A. C.: *Function of the human body.* Philadelphia: Saunders, 1959.

Holding, T., & Minkoff, K.: Parasuicide and the menstrual cycle. *Journal of Psychosomatic Research,* 17: 365-368, 1973.

Kane, F., Daly, R., Wallach, M., and Keeler, M.: Amelioration of premenstrual mood disturbance with a progestational agent. *Diseases of the Nervous System,* 27: 339-342, 1966.

Lester, D.: The antisuicide pill. *Journal of the American Medical Association,* 208: 1908, 1969.

Lester, D.: *A physiological basis for personality traits.* Springfield: Thomas, 1974.

Lester, D.: Murder and suicide: are they polar opposites? *Behavioral Sciences & the Law,* 5: 49-60, 1987a.

Lester, D.: Comment on oral contraceptives, EEG dysrhythmias and suicide risk. *Clinical Electroencephalography,* 18: xiii, 1987b.

Lewis, G., & Fay, R.: Suicide in pregnancy. *British Journal of Clinical Practice,* 35: 51-53, 1981.

Mandell, A. J., & Mandell, M. P.: Suicide and the menstrual cycle. *Journal of the American Medical Association,* 200: 792-793, 1967.

McKinnon, I. L., McKinnon, P., & Thomson, A. D.: Lethal hazards of the luteal phase of the menstrual cycle. *British Medical Journal,* 1: 1015, 1959.

Pallis, D., & Holding, T.: The menstrual cycle and suicidal intent. *Journal of Biosocial Science,* 8: 27-33, 1976.

Rayburn, W., Aronow, R., Delancey, B., & Hogan, M.: Drug overdose during pregnancy. *Obstetrics & Gynecology,* 64: 611-614, 1984.

Ribeiro, A. L.: Menstruation and crime. *British Medical Journal,* 1: 640, 1962.

Roland, B. C., Morris, J. L., & Zelhart, P. F.: Proposed relation of testosterone levels to male suicides and sudden deaths. *Psychological Reports,* 59: 100-102, 1986.

Rosenberg, A. J., & Silver, E.: Suicide, psychiatrists and therapeutic abortion. *California Medicine,* 102: 407-411, 1965.

Rosenthal, R., Rinzler, C., Walsh, R., & Klausner, E.: Wrist-cutting syndrome. *American Journal of Psychiatry,* 128: 1363-1368, 1972.

Scott, J. P., & Fredericson, E.: The causes of fighting in mice and rats. *Physiological Zoology,* 24: 273-309, 1951.

Skutsch, G.: Manic depression. *Medical Hypotheses,* 7: 737-746, 1981.

Struve, F. A.: Possible potentiation of suicide risk in patients with EEG dysrhythmias taking oral contraceptives. *Clinical Electroencephalography,* 16: 88-90, 1985.

Tonks, C. M., Rack, P. H., & Rose, M. J.: Attempted suicide and the menstrual cycle. *Journal of Psychosomatic Research,* 2: 319-327, 1968.

Trautman, E. C.: The suicidal fit. *Archives of General Psychiatry,* 5: 76-83, 1961.

Vessey, M., McPherson, K., Lawless, M., & Yeates, D.: Oral contraception and serious psychiatric illness. *British Journal of Psychiatry,* 146: 45-49, 1985.

Wetzel, R. D., Reich, T., & McClure, J. N.: *The menstrual cycle, premenstrual symptoms, and self-callers to a suicide prevention service.* National Association for Mental Health, Washington, DC, 1969.

Wetzel, R., McClure, J., & Reich, T.: Premenstrual symptoms in self-referrals to a suicide prevention center. *British Journal of Psychiatry,* 119: 525-526, 1971a.

Wetzel, R., Reich, T., & McClure, J.: Phase of menstrual cycle and self-referrals to a suicide prevention center. *British Journal of Psychiatry,* 119: 523-524, 1971b.

Whitlock, F., and Edwards, J.: Pregnancy and attempted suicide. *Comprehensive Psychiatry,* 9: 1-12, 1968.

Winston, F.: Suicide and the menstrual cycle. *Journal of the American Medical Association,* 209: 1225, 1969.

CHAPTER 10

A PHYSIOLOGICAL THEORY
OF SEX DIFFERENCES IN SUICIDE

DAVID LESTER

SKUTSCH (1981a) has recently proposed a theory of depression based upon dopamine processes in the central nervous system. This chapter will first show that the theory receives support from studies of suicide and then apply the theory to explain the well known sex differences in suicide, namely that males complete suicide more whereas females attempt suicide more.

A DOPAMINE THEORY OF SUICIDE

Skutsch (1981a) proposed that those suffering from a psychotic depression have high levels of dopamine in their central nervous systems. A high level of dopamine in the central nervous system inhibits the output of aldosterone (a steroid produced by the adrenal cortex), leading to low levels of aldosterone in depressives. Dopamine also has natriuretic properties, leading to a low K^+/Na^+ ratio in the sweat of depressives.

In addition, Skutsch proposed that depressives have high levels of acetyl choline in their central nervous systems, which leads to abnormalities in the cortisol metabolism, namely, high basal cortisol levels and an insensitivity to dexamethazone suppression. These high levels of cortisol would be expected to lead to dilute sweat (that is, with a low concentration of salt), since cortisol has diuretic properties. (Aldosterone has anti-diuretic properties, thus also leading to dilute sweat in depressives.) The high levels of cortisol should also lead to high levels of 17-hydroxycorticosteroids (17-OHCS) in the urine of depressives.

119

EVIDENCE FROM STUDIES OF SUICIDE

Lester (1972, 1983) has reviewed research on the physiological characteristics of suicides.

Bunney and Fawcett (1965; Bunney, et al., 1969) have reported high levels of 17-OHCS in the urine of depressed completed and attempted suicides as compared to nonsuicidal depressed patients, although Krieger (1970) failed to replicate this finding.

Beskow, et al. (1976), however, found no consistent differences between the brains of suicides and controls in the concentration of dopamine.

Krieger (1970) found a higher level of cortisol in the blood of completed suicides as compared to controls. Platman, et al. (1971) noted an increase in plasma cortisol levels in one particular patient just before she attempted suicide. Although Brooksbank, et al. (1972) found no increase in cortisol levels in the brains of completed suicides as compared to those dying from other causes, an up-to-date review of the most recent research (Rich, 1986) concluded that elevation of cortisol levels does appear to be a fairly uniform finding of the research.

If a person is given a synthetic corticosteroid (such as dexamethasone) the pituitary stops its production of the adrenocorticotrophic hormone (ACTH), the hormone that controls the secretion of cortisol by the adrenals. Cortisol levels in the blood stay low for as long as eighteen hours, and this is the basis of the dexamethasone suppression test. It has been reported that depressed patients frequently fail to show this drop in cortisol levels after a dose of dexamethasone. Coryell and Schlesser (1981) presented evidence that suggested that suicide may be more common in those who have this abnormal response to dexamethasone.

Thus, the evidence from studies of suicides is quite supportive of Skutsch's domaminergic theory of depression.

THE ROLE OF ESTROGEN

Skutsch argued that estrogen suppresses dopamine release, leading to low levels of dopamine. She noted that estrogen levels are high during pregnancy, and drop almost to zero at parturition. Such a drop might also occur at menopause, after gonadectomy, and withdrawal from contraceptive pills.

In men, estrogen is derived from the peripheral conversion of testosterone. Thus, estrogen levels may reflect those of testosterone. Skutsch noted that testosterone levels are low in the Spring for men.

Since estrogens may be related to dopamine processes, this suggests that the dopaminergic theory of depression may provide an explanation for sex differences in suicidal behavior.

SEX DIFFERENCES IN SUICIDAL BEHAVIOR

The most obvious sex difference in suicidal behavior is that men complete suicide more than women while women attempt suicide more than men. Lester (1979) documented the generality of this phenomenon in all groups in the USA and also around the world. Although some investigators argue that the difference in the lethality of the methods chosen by men and women accounts for the phenomenon, Lester (1969a) showed that, within any method for suicide, the same phenomenon is found—the men die more and the women survive more.

Lester (1984) noted that while research showed that the completed suicide rate did not seem to vary consistently over the menstrual cycle of women, attempted suicide was more common during the premenstrual and bleeding phases. During these phases, the estrogen level is low (Guyton, 1959). According to Skutsch's theory of depression, this should lead to higher levels of dopamine and thus increased depression. This would be consistent with higher rates of attempted suicide.

Pregnant women have a low rate of suicide, while attempted suicide seems to occur at a normal rate. During pregnancy, estrogen levels are low, and so dopamine levels should be high and depression more likely. Thus, suicidal behavior in pregnant women does not support the proposed theory.

Kane, et al. (1966) reported on the use of Enovid (a synthetic hormone preparation) to treat the symptoms of a suicidal psychotic female, and this would make sense according to the dopaminergic theory. The estrogen would suppress the levels of dopamine, thereby decreasing the depression. Lester (1969b) suggested that women on contraceptive pills should have their levels of hormones affected by the pill, and thus their suicidal behavior might also be affected.

Skutsch (1981b) noted that the highest levels of cortisol occur in January and February (in the Northern Hemisphere) whereas aldosterone levels are low in winter and peak in April and May. She suggested that dopamine is sensitive to temperature. The early summer leads to a drop in dopamine levels, which triggers a rise in aldosterone levels. Skutsch used this to account for the fact that the suicide rates for women peaked in the Spring and the Fall, unlike those for men which showed only a Spring peak. (She suggested that the secondary peak in the Fall for women might be accounted for the annual variation in the levels of circulating estrogens.)

Conclusions

Although Skutsch's theory of depression is speculative at the moment, the relationship between estrogens and dopamine levels provides a new way of accounting for sex differences in suicidal behavior. Previous theories of this sex difference in suicidal behavior focussed on differences in choice of method for suicide and on the societal knowledge that attempted suicide was a "feminine" act, making it less of an alternative for men. Although estrogens were thought to be related to suicidal behavior, no mechanism that would account for this association had previously been proposed. The present theory may prove heuristic for future research.

REFERENCES

Beskow, J., Gottfries, C., Roos, B., & Winblad, B.: Determinants of monoamine metabolites in the human brain. *Acta Psychiatrica Scandinavia*, 53: 7-20, 1976.

Brooksbank, B., Brammall, M., Cunningham, A., Shaw, D., & Camps, F. Estimation of corticosteroids in human cerebral cortex after death by suicide, accident or disease. *Psychological Medicine*, 2: 56-65, 1972.

Bunney, W., & Fawcett, J.: Possibility of a biochemical test for suicide potential. *Archives of General Psychiatry*, 13: 232-239, 1965.

Bunney, W., Fawcett, J., Davis, J., & Gifford, S.: Further evaluation of urinary 17-hydrocorticosteroids in suicidal patients. *Archives of General Psychiatry*, 21: 138-150, 1969.

Coryell, W., & Schlesser, M.: Suicide and the dexamethasone suppression test. *American Journal of Psychiatry*, 138: 1120-1121, 1981.

Guyton, A.: *Functions of the human body*. Philadelphia: Saunders, 1959.

Kane, F., Daly, R., Wallach, M., & Keeler, M.: Amelioration of premenstrual mood disturbance with a progestational agent. *Diseases of the Nervous System*, 27: 339-342, 1966.

Krieger, G.: Biochemical predictors of suicide. *Diseases of the Nervous System*, 31: 479-482, 1970.

Lester, D.: Suicidal behavior in men and women. *Mental Hygiene,* 53: 340-345, 1969a.

Lester, D.: The anti-suicide pill. *Journal of the American Medical Association,* 208: 1980, 1969b.

Lester, D.: *Why people kill themselves.* Springfield: Thomas, 1972.

Lester, D.: Sex differences in suicidal behavior. In E. Gomberg & V. Franks (Eds.) *Gender and disordered behavior.* New York: Brunner/Mazel, 1979.

Lester, D.: *Why people kill themselves.* 2nd. ed. Springfield: Thomas, 1983.

Lester, D.: Suicide. In C. Widom (Ed.) *Sex roles and psychopathology.* New York: Plenum, 1984.

Platman, S., Plutchik, R., & Weinstein, B.: Psychiatric, physiological, behavioral and self-report measures in relation to suicide attempt. *Journal of Psychiatric Research,* 8: 127-137, 1971.

Rich, C.: Endocrinology and suicide. *Suicide & Life-Threatening Behavior,* 16: 301-311, 1986.

Skutsch, G.: Manic depression. *Medical Hypotheses,* 7: 737-746, 1981a.

Skutsch, G.: Sex differences in seasonal variations in suicide rate. *British Journal of Psychiatry,* 139: 80-81, 1981.

CHAPTER 11

VIRGINIA WOOLF: THE LIFE
OF A COMPLETED SUICIDE

DAVID LESTER

VIRGINIA WOOLF was a leading literary figure in Great Britain in the early part of this century. She wrote novels, book reviews for newspapers and magazines and literary criticism. She drowned herself in the River Ouse on March 28th, 1941 at the age of 59. The present chapter is based on a biography written by her nephew, Quentin Bell (1972).

Her Parents and Early Years

The Stephens were originally a family of farmers and merchants from Aberdeenshire in Scotland. Her grandfather was first a lawyer, but then joined the Civil Service in the Colonial Office, working hard for the abolition of slavery. He wrote, particularly for the *Edinburgh Review*. He was shy, pessimistic, convinced of his ugliness, and prone to deny himself any pleasure. If he found something he liked (like cigars or snuff), he avoided it altogether.

His youngest surviving child was a son, Leslie. Leslie was a nervous delicate boy, his mother's darling, and fond of poetry. He went to Cambridge University and later accepted a fellowship there, becoming an ordained minister in the process which was a pre-requisite for the position. However, he was dissatisfied by the life there and moved to London where he worked as a journalist. He eventually became editor of the *Dictionary of National Biography*.

His first wife was Harriet Thackeray, daughter of the novelist. They had a daughter, Laura, who was soon noticed to be psychologically disturbed.[1] Harriet died in childbirth in 1875, on Leslie's forty-third birthday. Leslie soon became close to a friend of his wife, Julia Jackson (Duckworth), recently widowed and with three children. They married on March 26, 1878.

They already had four children by their first spouses, and they had two more, a daughter Vanessa and a son Thoby. They planned no more children, but had two more anyway, Virginia and Adrian.

Virginia was born January 25, 1882 in London, into the upper middle classes, though Bell sees the family as at the lower division of this particular class. They had seven maidservants but no manservants. They sometimes traveled in a cab but did not keep a carriage.

Virginia was a pretty child and, though she was slow in learning to talk, soon showed a precocious brilliance. The children soon decided that Vanessa would be a painter and Virginia a writer. Virginia was later described as eccentric, prone to accidents, witty and easily provoked to furious rages by her brothers and sisters.

Childhood was relatively uneventful. They all got whooping cough in 1888, from which they all recovered, though Virginia seemed weaker afterwards. The boys were sent off to school, while the girls were educated at home by their parents and then by a succession of governesses and tutors. They learned drawing, dancing, music, and languages. They vacationed in St Ives, Cornwall.

Virginia, who had become the story teller in the nursery, started a family newspaper in 1891 which she produced weekly for four years.

Since we know that Virginia eventually became psychiatrically disturbed, it is important to look for portents of madness in the family. In 1891, Laura was still living at home. A cousin, J. K. Stephen, received brain damage in an accident in 1886 and subsequently showed signs of madness, in particular manic euphoria and excitement.

Virginia's father had very poor health. He collapsed in 1888, 1890, and 1891. He suffered from insomnia, what he called "fits of the horrors," and worries about his finances.

In 1895, Virginia's mother caught influenza. It was followed by rheumatic fever, and she died on May 5th, 1895. Virginia was thirteen. Her father was sixty-three, a widower for the second time. His grief was great, and he broke down frequently in front of his children. His

---

1. She died in an asylum in 1945.

step-daughter, Stella, stepped in to take over the family and comfort Leslie. The oldest of the step-children, George, now twenty-seven, began at this time to molest Virginia (and continued to do so until she was twenty-two).

Adolescence and the First Breakdown

Virginia's first 'breakdown' occurred in the summer of 1895, soon after her mother's death. Later she remembered the excitability and nervousness, intolerable depression, a fear of meeting people and hearing voices. She stopped writing her family newspaper.

Stella became engaged in 1896 and was married in April, 1897. She became ill with peritonitis and died in July. Virginia's health deteriorated during this period. There was a fear of going out in the street, and also a fever and rheumatic pains. But there was not a complete breakdown. Soon she was back at lessons, learning Greek and Latin.

Leslie's hearing was deteriorating and a lot of his friends had died. However, he had recovered from his grief, though he remained chronically melancholy. He encouraged the literary interests of his family and turned to Vanessa to run the family. He continued to worry about finances which made life hard for Vanessa who had to fight with him for money to run the household.

Thoby went to Cambridge, and Vanessa and Virginia were introduced to his friends, many of whom later became the nucleus of an intellectual group centered around the Stephens children and known as the Bloomsbury group. Vanessa made more of an effort to "come out" in society than Virginia, but both thoroughly disliked this and withdrew from the activities as soon as they could.

On Their Own as Adults

Leslie died after a long illness in February 1904. In May, Virginia had her second breakdown. She heard voices, distrusted Stella and her nurses, tried to starve herself and grieved for her father. She tried to kill herself by jumping from a window which was not high enough for her to do much harm. As she recovered, the mental symptoms lessened, leaving her with headaches and neuralgia.

The three children decided to move into a house in Bloomsbury by themselves. They began to have "At Homes" on Thursday evenings to which many intellectual friends came. Virginia published her first piece in *The Guardian* at the end of 1904, and in 1905 she began her association with *The Times Literary Supplement.* She taught briefly at an evening institute for working men. Then in 1906 on a trip to Greece, Vanessa and Thoby both became ill. Vanessa recovered, but Thoby was misdiagnosed as having malaria and died in November with typhoid fever. Vanessa became engaged to Clive Bell two days later. Interestingly during these crises, Virginia functioned well and without any breakdown, though she missed Thoby greatly.

After Vanessa's marriage. Virginia and Adrian moved into a smaller house, and their life continued much as before with Thoby's friends as theirs and with activities being split between their household and the Bell's. Virginia's writing was successful, and she began working on a novel in addition to writing for literary magazines. Virginia also began seriously to think of marriage for the first time.

Hitherto, Virginia had been attached mainly to women, especially Violet Dickinson, who seemed to have been in love with Virginia and vice versa, though the relationship was not sexual. Virginia's first flirtation was with an older family friend, Walter Headlam, but the interest soon petered out, and he died unexpectedly in June 1908, causing her some grief.

Virginia was physically ill and close to another breakdown in 1910 but recovered after a rest cure. She turned down a proposal of marriage from Lytton Strachey (who was homosexual[2]) and resisted the attention of her brother-in-law, Clive. After rejecting several suitors, in 1911, an old friend, Leonard Woolf, returned on leave from Ceylon and fell in love with Virginia. After another bout with exhaustion in 1912, Virginia agreed to marry Leonard. The wedding took place in August, 1912.

Mrs. Woolf

Virginia's life with Leonard was full, but also relatively uneventful. They lived happily together, moved houses, started a publishing company (the Hogarth Press), and worked hard. Virginia wrote and wrote, eventually amassing a considerable body of work, including novels that were received with critical acclaim.

Their life quickly developed into a routine. Leonard took care of Virginia a lot, especially during her breakdowns, but also between

---

2. Many of the men in the Bloomsbury circle were gay, and Virginia's attraction to them may have been increased by her fear of (and inexperience with) sex, sensitized as she had been by her earlier experiences of sexual molestation.

breakdowns as he tried to prevent their reoccurrence. They wrote most mornings, walked in the afternoons, and read in the evenings. They entertained a lot and were entertained in return.

Virginia was frigid, which everyone ascribed to her experiences with her half-brother. Virginia wanted to have children, though Leonard did not. After much consultation with specialists, the majority opinion was that it was too dangerous for her to have any.

Her first novel *(The Voyage Out)* was accepted in 1913, though it was not published until March 1915. However, its acceptance led to another breakdown. She had anxieties about her writing talent, sleepless nights, headaches, depression, a sense of guilt, an aversion to food, and fears that people were laughing at her. In September, 1913, Virginia took a lethal dose of veronal, but after having her stomach pumped, she survived—barely. As she recovered, her manias returned, and she went from depression to violent excitement.[3] Leonard considered putting her into an asylum, but rejected the idea, and slowly she began to recover, though with a relapse in February, 1915 just before her novel appeared.

The reviews of her novel were positive, and her recovery progressed. Virginia's novels were very close to her own private world, and she was aware that they might be seen as crazy (or really be crazy). If they had been mocked, then this would have been a mockery of her true self. Praise for her novels was a certificate of sanity.

Her Death

Virginia had breakdowns in June 1921 (after a mild depression in August 1919 just before the publication of *Night and Day*), and mild ones in August 1926, September 1929, May 1936. She had frequent periods of total exhaustion, notably January, 1922, September, 1925, and July, 1933, as well as many less severe illnesses.[4]

All of her novels caused her anxiety and depression, especially during the time between the completion of writing and the appearance of the book. Also, beginning in 1934, her style was seen by critics as old-fashioned, and criticism became more common.

---

3. Leonard, and others, later diagnosed Virginia's disorder as manic-depressive psychosis.

4. September 1922, January, 1923, January, 1925, January, 1926, June, 1927, January, 1928, January, 1929, February, 1930, August, 1930, May, 1931, November, 1931, July, 1932, November, 1932, February, 1934, May, 1934, October, 1934, January, 1936, November, 1937, January, 1938, April, 1939, and February, 1940. Many of these illnesses were accompanied by or the result of Winter influenzas.

As she grew older, more and more friends died. Kitty Maxse killed herself in 1922 and Dora Carrington in 1932. Lytton Strachey died in 1932 and her nephew Julian in 1937 in the Spanish Civil War.

The Second World War also created intense stress for Virginia. (Leonard was Jewish.) They discussed suicide in May, 1940, and decided to keep enough gasoline on hand (and later morphia) to kill themselves.

She finished a final novel *(Between the Acts)* in November 1940. By January, Leonard was alarmed at her psychological state. On the morning of Friday, March 28, 1941, Virginia wrote suicide notes and walked to the River Ouse where she put a large stone into her coat pocket and drowned herself (perhaps already having tried to drown herself one time before). In her letter to Leonard, she explained:

> I feel certain I am going mad again. I feel we can't go through another of those terrible times. And I shan't recover this time. (Bell, 1972, p. 226)

Analysis

Virginia clearly had recurrent mental breakdowns during her life. It is possible that she indeed suffered from a manic-depressive psychosis, with periods of depression and mania. She also heard voices and had some phobic behaviors concerned with eating (even when she was not psychotic).

Her breakdowns seemed to have occurred after two types of events: severe loss (for example, after the death of her mother) and after completing a novel and waiting for its publication.

She was also prone to exhaustion, and her family thought that this was brought on by too much social activity. Typically, a rest cure was prescribed. This exhaustion seemed to facilitate the appearance of a breakdown.

Her suicide note asserts that she is killing herself because she is scared of suffering another breakdown, one with no recovery, and because of the effect of her illnesses on Leonard. Some people go mad to prevent themselves committing suicide; others commit suicide because of their fear of mental illness. Virginia was clearly among the latter.

The question that remains is one of timing. Why in 1941? Yet she almost died in her suicide attempt soon after her marriage, when her literary career was still in its infancy. By 1941, however, her novels were receiving increasing criticism, and she feared that she would not be able to write again. The war, with its threats for Leonard, was also a new stress. (Their house in London was damaged by bombs.) She was fifty-nine, perhaps no longer possessing the resiliency of her youth.

She was an agnostic, without religious beliefs that might inhibit her taking her own life. This time, too, there was no attending physician to advise them. Leonard persuaded a friend who was a physician to see Virginia. She did so, though she was physically ill herself. But apart from this one consultation, there was no doctor, therapist or nurse on hand. Four days before her suicide, Virginia wrote to her publishers, asking that her novel not be published, indicating that her typical fears about publishing were still strong.

If she had been able to survive this latest breakdown, would she have recovered as she had in the past? And would she eventually have killed herself, perhaps during the next crisis. She was a chronically depressed person, with a history of suicidal preoccupation, and she might have killed herself at any time. It is perhaps a surprise that she lived so long.

REFERENCE

Bell, Q. *Virginia Woolf.* New York: Harcourt Brace Jovanovich, 1972.

CHAPTER 12

DOROTHY PARKER: THE LIFE
OF AN ATTEMPTED SUICIDE

DAVID LESTER

LESTER (1987) has studied the lives of famous people who killed themselves, people such as Ernest Hemingway and Marilyn Monroe. Sometimes it is easy to pick out childhood experiences, personality traits and life-style factors that seem to be portents of the later suicide.

But as we have seen in this book, suicide in women involves attempted suicide more often than completed suicide. Can we take the life of an attempted suicide and, not only pick out those factors that seem to be portents of the attempts, but also discover factors that explain why the person did *not* eventually kill herself?

To do this, I am going to take Dorothy Parker who attempted suicide at least twice in her life, yet died at the age of seventy-three from a heart attack. I will first present a brief biography of Dorothy (based on Keats, 1970) and then discuss the psychological features of interest about her life. Finally, I will compare her life with those of the famous women who completed suicide, Virginia Woolf, living during the same period but in England, and Marilyn Monroe, a generation later in America.

Dorothy's Early Years

Dorothy was born on August 22, 1893 to Mrs. Henry Rothschild. Unfortunately, Mrs. Rothschild was on holiday at the New Jersey shore at the time, and Dorothy was two months premature.

The Rothschilds were not related to *the* Rothschilds, although Mr. Rothschild had been successful in the garment industry and lived in a good neighborhood in the West Seventies in Manhattan, waited on by servants. Mr. Rothschild was Jewish, but his wife was Scottish.

Dorothy found no love in her home. She had an older sister and an older brother but seems not to have been close to them. Her mother died during her infancy. Her father remarried, but Dorothy never felt close to or liked her stepmother. She also seems to have been terrified of her father.

Her stepmother was Catholic and took pains to have Dorothy brought up as a Catholic. She sent her to nearby Catholic school run by nuns where Dorothy felt like an outsider. Dorothy hated being a Jew. She hated her name, and she grew to hate herself.

Dorothy developed two sides to her personality. Outwardly, she became well-mannered, pretty (with beautiful dark hair and large eyes that seemed close to tears), the feminine dissembler. Inside was an angry, truth-seeking rebellious mind, appraising the world with ruthless accuracy.

For high school, she was fortunate in being sent to Miss Dana's School in Morristown, New Jersey. It was one of the best boarding schools in the nation. Leading women's colleges waived the examination requirement for students from the school. Although after graduation in 1911 Dorothy did not go to college, she acquired a sound education while at the school, not only in classical studies but in current affairs.

The Young Adult

Dorothy's first few years after high school are not well documented. Her father died when she was nineteen. Soon after leaving high school, she found herself a room in a boarding house in Manhattan. She also spent some time writing and supported herself by playing the piano for a dancing school.

She had a poem accepted by *Vogue* in 1916, and the editor gave her a job. Now her days were full. She had two jobs and continued to write and submit her poems. In 1917 she was promoted to *Vanity Fair,* and she also married Edwin Parker.

Edwin Parker worked as a broker in Wall Street. He was an Anglo-Saxon Protestant from an old, religious Hartford family, and they were in love. However, on March 4, 1917 America declared war on Germany, and Eddie enlisted, ending up in the ambulance corps.

While he was in America, Dorothy visited him on weekends at the camps where he was, or Eddie would come to Manhattan. But then, eventually he was sent to Europe. Their marriage had consisted of nine months of weekends and then letter-writing. Dorothy wrote to him every day. After the war, Eddie was assigned to occupation duty in the Rhineland.

Meanwhile, Robert Benchley and Robert Sherwood joined *Vanity Fair*, and Dorothy would go with them for lunch to the Algonquin Hotel, starting a lunch group of talented young men and women that over the years became famous (later including Franklin Pierce Adams, Alexander Woollcott and Harold Ross).

This group helped the metamorphosis of Dorothy. In 1919, there was no radio or television, and so newspapers were widely read and very influential. Adams's column was one of the most popular newspaper columns, and he began to report on Dorothy's witticisms at lunch (and her evening outings) to his readers. Soon Dorothy Parker had a reputation as the wittiest woman in New York. This reputation, combined with a life-style in which she smoked, worked for a living, took lunch and went unchaperoned to the theater with other women's husbands, also set her apart as one of the New Women.

The Algonquin group did not discuss each other's work. Their conversation was witty and superficial. They went to parties, the theater and speakeasies. Unlike those leading a Bohemian life, the group was not revolting against society — they felt superior to it. Of course, the wittiness was often hostile, especially toward those who were not with the group at the time. The humor turned to banter, and the banter to insult.

Eddie returned in August, 1919, after a separation of fifteen months. He did not fit in well with the Algonquin crowd, and he soon began to drop out of the social life of the group. By 1920, Eddie was drinking heavily. He wanted to move back to Hartford, but Dorothy refused. She loved life in New York and felt that her in-laws disliked her for having a Jewish father. She soon moved out to her own apartment. (Eddie permitted Dorothy to divorce him in Connecticut for cruelty, in 1926, and to retain his name.)

Dorothy was fired early in 1920 from *Vanity Fair*, and the two Roberts (Benchley and Sherwood) resigned in protest. They soon got other jobs, but Dorothy remained unemployed. She also seemed to have stopped writing. (It always seemed to others that writing was a distasteful chore for Dorothy.) Nothing appeared in 1920 or 1921. But in 1922 she fell in love again.

Unfortunately, she fell in love with Charles MacArthur, a young newspaperman and a womanizer. But now her writing could proceed again. Her pieces appeared in the leading magazines, and she and friends wrote a revue *(No, Siree!)* that ran for a month.

As her relationship with Charles began to ebb, she discovered she was pregnant. She had an abortion, and soon after attempted suicide. She was at home in her apartment and asked for food to be sent up. When the waiter arrived, he found her in the bathroom with her wrists slashed. Some of her friends thought she intended this as a gesture; others thought it was a sign of her disorganization and impulsiveness. After this, she began to drink more.

At thirty, Dorothy was still beautiful. She was also neither married, divorced, nor celibate. She lived in a cheap apartment building, with no close female friends. (Later in life, she would be close to Beatrice Ames and a few other women.) She was witty and a good writer, but in 1924 she hardly wrote.

By 1925 she was writing the poems that would be in her first book, *Enough Rope,* some sweet and poignant, others flippant and ironic, ranging from black to blue. But she also attempted suicide again, this time more seriously. Robert Benchley and others found her in her apartment, comatose from an overdose of drugs.

One of her stanzas from this period is:

> If wild my breast and sore my pride,
> I bask in dreams of suicide;
> If cool my heart and high my head,
> I think, "How lucky are the dead!"

Her next lover was Seward Collins, heir to a national chain of tobacco shops, a patron of the arts who adored her. In 1926 they went to France to meet the American intellectuals in Paris, ending up with the Murphy's on the French Riviera. Dorothy and Seward quarelled during the trip, and Seward left for America. Dorothy stayed on 'till October, arriving home with a best selling book — of poems no less. Soon she was an enormous success, contributing to *The New Yorker* and *The Bookman,* well-publicized and talked-about.

Dorothy began to tire a little of her group. It seemed trivial; it lacked any meaning. She began to get involved with political issues, supporting Sacco and Vanzetti, anarchists accused of murdering during a payroll robbery. They were executed on her thirty-fourth birthday. In 1928, her second book of poems was published, and she was involved with a businessman, John Garrett. But she was beginning to write the short stories on which her claim to literary stature would be based. "Big Blonde" won the national O. Henry Prize as the best short story in 1929.

She next had an affair with John McClain, a clerk on Wall Street, had an appendectomy which, despite her income, she couldn't pay for. (Dorothy always had to rely on her friends to manage her life.) She pursued gaiety and drank heavily. (She even went to Alcoholics Anonymous for one meeting, and her biographer, Keats, considers Dorothy to have been an alcoholic in the modern sense of the word.)

Life with Alan

In 1932, Dorothy met Alan Campbell. In 1933 she married him. He was twenty-nine and she was forty. Alan was also half Jewish and half Scottish. Alan was a minor actor, aware that his talents were meager. He had hopes of taking Dorothy to Hollywood where they could work together on movie scripts.

Life with Alan soon fell into a pattern. They had fun but quarelled a lot. They even got divorced for one period but remarried. They worked well together on scripts. Between 1933 and 1938, they received screen credits for fifteen films, including "A Star Is Born" and earned lots of money that they quickly spent. They drank heavily, and Dorothy put on weight.

Alan liked Hollywood, but Dorothy did not. This led to frequent sojourns to New York, followed by trips back to Hollywood. For a while they owned a house in Bucks County, near Philadelphia (where she miscarried after three months of pregnancy), and commuted across country to Hollywood.

Although Dorothy said that she was happy during this time, Keats describes her as " . . . living with a fretful husband in a rather oddly furnished house, quarreling with her friends, allowing herself to grow dumpy in barren middle age, wasting her time on silly scripts, stunning herself with alcohol and sleeping pills . . . "

Dorothy took up the anti-Nazi cause in the Spanish Civil War, even calling herself a communist. She went to Spain in 1937 to view the war from the Loyalist side. (The result, of course, was the blacklisting of both her and Alan in the 1940s, and even more so in the 1950s during America's hysterical anti-communist witch-hunt.)

Alan joined the Air Force, and Dorothy was both proud of him and scared of him going off to war as Eddie had in the First World War. She followed Alan from camp to camp in America, as she had with Eddie, until he was sent to Europe. After victory, Alan stayed in London. Dorothy told friends he was involved in a homosexual affair. (She had accused him of homosexual leanings throughout their marriage.) And she divorced him.

But this time, there were no suicide attempts.

Dorothy published nothing in 1945 and 1946. But after the divorce in 1947, she collaborated on a story, a play and a film script with her lover (Ross Evans). In 1949, after being dumped by Ross, she called Alan who had returned to Hollywood, and they decided to get back together.

After they remarried in 1950, they lived in Hollywood, but they separated after two years, and Dorothy went back to New York, where she lived at the Volney Hotel with other lonely aging ladies. But three years later, Alan visited her in New York and persuaded her to return to Hollywood to work on a movie script with him. The movie was never produced, and that was the last script they ever worked on. They lived on their unemployment checks (of $300 a month each) until Dorothy was hired by *Esquire* to write book reviews for $750 a month. (*Esquire* continued to pay her this each month until she died, regardless of whether she sent them any reviews.)[1]

After seven years in their small house in a seedy section of Los Angeles, Dorothy woke up one morning, to find Alan dead beside her. June 13, 1963. Dorothy was sixty-nine. She returned to New York, to the Volney Hotel where she stayed until she died.

Her last article appeared in the November, 1964 issue of *Esquire*. She visited her old friend, Beatrice Ames, for dinners. Friends visited her but were often appalled by her alcohol abuse and the squalor of the rooms. She eventually began to lose her sight. She died at the age of seventy-three on June 7, 1967 of a heart attack.

Her death merited an obituary on Page 1 and almost all of Page 38 of *The New York Times.*

Discussion

Dorothy's early adult life in Manhattan and her public reputation as a witty, liberated woman obscured the other side of Dorothy. Her written work expressed the sadness over her life and her bitterness over the world, especially the lot of women. Despair lay behind most of her actions and

---

1. She did review 208 books for them, however.

writing. Her biographer describes her poems as " . . . portraying a woman who said she was suspicious of joy, disillusioned as to love, contemptuous of and sorry for herself, and given to thoughts of death."

Later, after twenty-nine so-so years with Alan, Keats describes her as " . . . crouched in silence, writing virtually nothing and drinking more than she ate, talking more to her poodle than with those who would be her friends, discontent with her present and dissatisfied with her memories of the past . . . "

Not a happy soul. Yet, she had a gritty determination to go on and could never quench her hope.

Her childhood was miserable. A mother dead early and a home with no love, only a harsh father and an eccentric step-mother. Schools where she felt an outsider. (She made no friends from those years, and her family had no place in her life.)

Her two suicide attempts (some friends reported at least five) were in her late twenties and early thirties. Charles MacArthur had abandoned her and left her to have an abortion prior to her first suicidal gesture. Her second attempt two years later was more serious, but Keats gives no immediate precipitating cause.

What is more curious is that in later life, romantic loss and living alone did not lead to suicide attempts. Her classic poem on methods of suicide had concluded that " . . . you might as well live." And so she did. But why?

Virginia Woolf

Virginia Woolf is an interesting person to compare with Dorothy Parker because they lived during the same time period and were both writers. They also were both centers of famous groups: for Dorothy the Algonquin group and for Virginia the Bloomsbury group.

The differences are immediately clear. Virginia had a much more stable home life, though she did lose her mother when she was thirteen. She married late in life, but had a stable and happy marriage (asexual though it might have been).

Virginia was much more of an intellectual than Dorothy. She wrote serious reviews of literature. She wrote novels that received critical acclaim rather than popular success. The Bloomsbury group discussed intellectual matters and was not simply a social group for witty repartee. Dorothy's was the life of those who ape the intellectuals, going to the theater, but not the symphony or the opera, drinking at speakeasies rather than gathering at friends' houses for talk.

With her husband, Virginia founded the Hogarth Press which published works such as those by Sigmund Freud. Dorothy and her husband wrote Hollywood scripts.

This is not to denigrate Dorothy. I was left with the feeling from the study of famous suicides that (some) intellectuals worry inordinately about issues that do not concern the rest of us. Some of them seemed to lack the capacity to enjoy life. Dorothy was not among those.

Dorothy's group reminded me of my immature years. I was part of a social group that tried to be humorous and witty. And I observed how such banter so easily turned hostile.[2] I found that being in such a social group engendered a cynical and hostile attitude toward the world, or nurtured the view that was already there. Since those early years, I have always avoided such groups.

But Dorothy was isolated from her family, without female friends, alone in New York. The Algonquin group was her only group.

Yet the most important difference between Virginia and Dorothy was that Virginia clearly had a bipolar affective disorder from an early age whereas Dorothy seemed to be free from psychiatric disorder. The more disturbed of the two made the more serious suicidal act.

Marilyn Monroe

Although Marilyn Monroe lived a generation after Dorothy, it is also interesting to compare her life with that of Dorothy.

Marilyn's childhood was much more disrupted than Dorothy's, though at each stop Marilyn probably had more friends and more affection than Dorothy had in her stable but awful home (Lester, 1987).

Like Dorothy, Marilyn's early suicide attempts were in response to loss of love. Like Dorothy, she drank heavily, but Marilyn abused prescription drugs more.

It is interesting to compare them in their thirties. Marilyn seems to be at the end of her career. She had been fired by the movie production company, she was divorced and about to be abandoned by her lover. Her beauty, which was the basis of her popularity, was going to be harder to maintain. Marilyn was at a choice point. She could not continue the old life and had to choose where to go. The options seemed limited. So she killed herself.

---

2. America is very fond of hostile humor, as illustrated by the success in the 1970s of comedians like Don Rickles and the televised "celebrity roasts."

Dorothy in her thirties was at the height of her literary fame. She was between husbands, but Alan was due to come along when she was thirty-nine. She was unhappy, as evidenced by her two suicide attempts. But her life was not at a point like Marilyn's. Dorothy, as far as she knew, was secure as a writer. She had published and would continue to do so. Her future writing might be worse, but it might be as good. Age would not affect her career. Dorothy had to make only minor adjustments.

Marilyn had a grandmother committed to a psychiatric hospital and a mother later committed to the same institution. Marilyn herself was also hospitalized. Marilyn may have had a genetic predisposition to affective disorder, whereas as we have already noted above, Dorothy was not as psychiatrically disturbed.

Conclusions

Perhaps the most surprising finding of this analysis has been the role of psychiatric disorder. Virginia Woolf and Marilyn Monroe were both psychiatrically disturbed. Although Marilyn's life seems to have been more traumatic than Dorothy's, Virginia's life does not.

Virginia killed herself because of her fear of mental illness. Marilyn Monroe killed herself because her life — at least the life she wanted — seemed over. But Dorothy lived on to an old age, not particularly happy but not too unhappy. At least the alcohol could blunt the pain of living. And for most of her middle and old age there was Alan to quarrel with and structure her life around. One *might* as well live.

REFERENCES

Keats, J.: *You might as well live.* New York: Simon & Schuster, 1970.

Lester, D.: Marilyn Monroe: love and loss in life. *Archives of the Foundation of Thanatology,* 13(4): unpaged, 1987.

NAME INDEX

A

Aass, G., 117
Akin, D., 88, 108
Allport, G., 53, 64
Angel, E., 51
Araki, S., 35, 40
Aronow, R., 118
Ayer, A., 64

B

Balance, W., 54, 65
Barnett, R., 40
Barno, A., 10, 14, 59, 64, 114, 117
Baruch, G., 38, 40
Beck, A., 8, 14
Bell, Q., 125, 130, 131
Berkowitz, L., 116, 117
Berman, P., 42
Berndt, R., 88, 108
Beskow, J., 120, 122
Biener, L., 40
Binswanger, L., 44, 51
Birtchnell, J., 112, 115, 117
Blachly, P., 37, 40
Bock, E., 6, 14
Brammall, M., 122
Brook, E., 41
Brooksbank, B., 120, 122
Broverman, D., 115, 117
Brown, M., 89, 108
Brown, P., 109
Buckle, R., 36, 41, 112, 117
Bunney, W., 120, 122
Burvill, P., 4, 14

C

Camps, F., 122

Carlson, G., 37, 41

Carlson, G., 37, 41
Carnap, R., 54, 64
Cawte, J., 88, 109
Chesler, P., 60, 65
Chisholm, L., 14
Cohen, S., 55, 56, 58, 59, 65
Colarusso, C., 56, 65
Cooper, M., 15
Coryell, W., 120, 122
Counts, D.A., 60, 65, 88, 94, 98, 100, 108, 109
Counts, D.R., 94, 100, 101, 108, 109
Craig, A., 37, 41
Cumming, E., 13, 14
Cunningham, A., 122

D

Dalton, K., 111, 117
Daly, R., 10, 15, 117, 122
Davis, F., 8, 14
Davis, J., 122
Davis, R., 39, 41, 44, 51, 59, 65
de Graaf, A., 3, 14
Delancey, B., 118
Dewhurst, W., 115, 117
Diggory, J., 9, 14, 33, 39, 41
Disher, W., 40
Durkheim, E., 6, 14, 35, 41

E

Edwards, J., 10, 15, 35, 42, 114, 118
Ekberg, O., 112, 117
Ellenberger, F., 51
Elliot, J., 60, 66
Epstein, A., 99, 109
Erikson, E., 56, 65
Estes, R., 21, 22
Eysenck, H., 116, 117

F

Farber, M., 36, 41
Farberow, N., 3, 8, 14, 44, 51, 52, 53, 54,
    55, 60, 66
Fawcett, J., 120, 122
Fay, R., 114, 118
Fiedler, J., 55, 56, 58, 59, 65
Finlay, S., 113, 117
Floyd, S., 112, 115, 117
Frankel, S., 89, 90, 109
Franks, V., 15, 66, 123
Frederick, C., 44, 51
Fredericson, E., 116, 118
Freeman-Browne, D., 41
Friedman, M., 88, 109

G

Gasner, S., 41
Geeken, M., 38, 41
Gegeo, D., 88, 109
Gibbs, J., 4, 14, 39, 41
Giddens, A., 87, 109
Gifford, S., 122
Gilligan, C., 60, 65
Glass, G., 112, 117
Goldberg, H., 60, 65
Gomberg, E., 15, 66, 123
Gottfries, C., 122
Gove, W., 4, 5, 6, 14, 15, 38, 41
Greenglass, E., 60, 65
Guyton, A., 114, 117, 121, 122

H

Hattem, J., 7, 15
Healey, C., 88, 109
Heilig, S., 44, 51
Heiman, M., 37, 41
Heninger, G., 117
Henry, A., 12, 15, 35, 41
Herman, J., 6, 15
Herold, J., 38, 42
Hezel, F., 108, 109
Hogan, M., 118
Holding, T., 112, 117, 118
Hoskins, J., 88, 109
Hudson, M., 21, 23

J

Jacobsen, D., 117
Jeffreys, M., 88, 89, 90, 109
Jewell, B., 59, 66
Johnson, P., 89, 90, 109

K

Kalish, R., 36, 41
Kane, F., 10, 15, 115, 117, 121, 122
Kayes, J., 41
Keats, J., 133, 141
Keeler, M., 10, 15, 117, 122
Kerlinger, F., 54, 65
Kessler, R., 5, 15
Kimmel, D., 56, 65
Klaiber, E., 117
Klausner, E., 118
Kobayashi, Y., 117
Kovacs, M., 14
Krieger, G., 120, 122
Kruyt, C., 3, 14

L

Lansky, M., 117
Lawless, M., 15, 118
Lazer, C., 14
Leenaars, A., 53, 54, 55, 56, 58, 59, 60, 61, 65
Lemkau, P., 10, 15
Lester, D., 3, 4, 7, 9, 10, 12, 14, 15, 19, 20,
    22, 26, 33, 37, 39, 40, 41, 42, 55, 56,
    58, 59, 61, 65, 66, 115, 116, 117, 118,
    120, 121, 123, 133, 140, 141
Lettieri, D., 44, 46, 52
Levenson, M., 51, 52
Lewis, G., 114, 118
Li, F., 37, 41
Linane, J., 41, 117
Linehan, M., 10, 15, 59, 66
Litman, R., 44, 50, 51
London, J., 38, 41
Luton, F., 10, 15
Lynn, R., 21, 22

M

Mandell, A., 111, 118
Mandell, M., 111, 118

Maris, R., 36, 41, 53, 60, 61, 66
Marks, A., 9, 15
Marshall, M., 88, 109
Martin, W., 4, 14, 39, 41
Mausner, J., 37, 42
May, R., 51
McClure, J., 118
McConaghy, N., 41, 117
McIntosh, J., 59, 66
McKellin, W., 88, 109
McKinnon, I., 113, 118
McKinnon, P., 118
McPherson, K., 15, 118
McRae, J., 5, 15
Merikangas, K., 38, 41
Michelson, W., 38, 41
Micklin, M., 39, 41
Miley, J., 39, 41
Miller, D., 37, 41
Minkoff, K., 112, 117
Moore, J., 37, 42
Morris, J., 118
Mortimer, J., 38, 41
Murata, K., 40
Murphy, G., 41

N

Nemiroff, R., 56, 65
Neuringer, C., 43, 44, 46, 47, 51, 52
Newman, H., 15, 41
Newman, J., 12, 15, 39, 41

O

O'Brien, D., 108
Ornstein, M., 59, 66
Osgood, C., 43

P

Pallis, D., 112, 118
Panoff, M., 90, 109
Peck, M., 51
Pitts, A., 41
Pitts, F., 37, 41
Platman, S., 120, 123
Platt, S., 36, 41
Pleck, J., 38, 42
Plutchik, R., 123
Poole, F., 88, 109

R

Rack, P., 118
Ramey, E., 42
Rayburn, W., 114, 118
Reay, M., 89, 109
Reeve, C., 55, 56, 58, 59, 66
Reich, T., 118
Ribeiro, A., 113, 118
Rich, C., 41, 120, 123
Rinzler, C., 118
Robin, A., 35, 41
Robins, E., 41
Roduner, G., 40
Roland, B., 114, 118
Roos, B., 122
Rose, K., 37, 41
Rose, M., 118
Rosenberg, A., 114, 118
Rosenthal, R., 113, 118
Rosow, I., 37, 41
Ross, M., 4, 15
Roth, W., 10, 15
Rothman, D., 9, 14
Rubinstein, D., 108, 109
Rudzinski, D., 54, 65
Runyan, W., 53, 66
Rushing, W., 36, 41

S

Schapira, K., 35, 42
Schlesser, M., 120, 122
Scholler, A., 41
Scott, J., 116, 118
Shaw, D., 122
Shneidman, E., 3, 14, 43, 52, 53, 54, 55, 58, 60, 61, 65, 66
Shontz, F., 45, 52
Short, J., 12, 15, 35, 41
Siegel, S., 66
Silver, E., 114, 118
Simon, J., 35, 42
Sivers, H., 88, 109
Skutsch, G., 115, 118, 119, 121, 123
Sorum, Y., 117
Stack, S., 12, 15, 20, 21, 22, 23, 27, 33, 39, 42
Staines, G., 38, 42
Steffensmeier, R., 38, 42

Stengel, E., 36, 42, 60, 66
Stephens, B., 85
Steppacher, R., 37, 42
Stewart, A., 11, 15, 20, 21, 23
Stokes, C., 9, 15
Strathen, A., 89, 109
Strathen, M., 89, 109
Struve, F., 115, 118

T

Talan, K., 117
Taylor, C., 21, 23
Thomson, A., 118
Tietze, C., 15
Tiffany, S., 108
Tomlinson-Keasey, C., 60, 66
Tonks, C., 111, 118
Trautman, E., 111, 118
Tuckman, J., 35, 36, 42
Tuzin, D., 101, 109

V

Verbrugge, L., 38, 42
Vessey, M., 10, 15, 115, 118
Vogel, W., 117
Voydanoff, P., 41

W

Waldron, I., 38, 42

Walker, E., 43
Wallach, M., 10, 15, 117, 122
Walsh, R., 118
Warren, L., 60, 66
Watson-Gegeo, K., 88, 109
Webber, I., 6, 14
Weinstein, B., 123
Wenckstern, S., 54, 65
Wetzel, R., 111, 113, 118
White, G., 108, 109
Whitlock, F., 10, 15, 35, 42, 114, 118
Whittemore, K., 15, 41
Widom, C., 15, 66, 123
Wilkinson, R., 41
Winblad, B., 122
Windelband, W., 53, 66
Winston, F., 115, 118
Winter, D., 11, 15, 20, 21, 23
Wold, C., 7, 15
Wolff, H., 54, 66

Y

Yap, P., 3, 15
Yeates, D., 15, 118
Yeh, B., 40, 42
Youngman, W., 35, 42

Z

Zelhart, P., 118
Zung, W., 37, 42

SUBJECT INDEX

A

Abuse, childhood, 76
Abuse and battering, 82, 90, 91
Acetyl choline, 119
Age, 4, 19
Alcoholic parents, 77
Aldosterone, 119, 121
Anorexia, 79
Attitudes toward death, 9, 44, 45
Autonomic nervous system, 116

B

Birth control, 112
Birth control pill, 115, 120, 121

C

Chemists, 37
Childhood, 75
Cognition, 43
Community surveys, 3
Cortisol, 119
Crisis workers, 37

D

Depression, 115
Dexamethasone suppression, 119
Dichotomous thinking, 43
Divorce, 20
Dopamine, 115, 119
Dysmenorrhea, 112, 113

E

Economic development, 19

Economy, 35
EEG, paroxysmal, 115
Employment, 13
Era, 4, 38
Estrogen, 114, 115, 116, 120

F

Females in labor force, 39
Firearms, 9
First-borns, 94

H

Hong Kong, 3

I

Incest, 82
Industrialization, 20
Inequality, sexual, 11, 20
Infidelity, 82
International statistics, 17
Interpersonal factors, 73

L

Labor force, 12, 30
Loss, early, 76

M

Marital status, 5, 13
Menopause, 115, 120
Menstruation, 9, 111
Mental illness (in parents), 76
Methods for suicide, 8

147

N

Neglect (childhood), 75
Netherlands, 3
Neurosis, 10

O

Occupational status, 36

P

Papua, 87
Parents, 75
Parker, D., 133
Physicians, 4, 36
Police officers, 37
Polygyny, 94
Pregnancy, 10, 112, 120
Professionals, 4, 36
Psychosis, 10

R

Race, 4
Revenge suicide, 88
Role conflict, 73
Roles, 12, 77

S

Season, 121
Self-esteem, 75

Self-immolation, 113
Self-mutilation, 79
17-OHCS, 119
Sex hormones, 10, 114
Sex roles, 7
Shame, 88
Social isolation, 75
Societal expectations, 10
States, 25
Status, 12
Suicidal intent, 9
Suicide as homicide, 98
  as play, 88
  as a political act, 93
  as a social sanction, 88
Suicide notes, 43, 53
Suicide prevention, 49, 50

T

Testosterone, 114, 121
Typtophan, 115

U

Unemployment, 35

W

War, 12
Widowhood, 6
Woolf, V., 125
Working women, 38
Wrist-cutters, 113